Robert Jackson is a professional aviation and military historian. He has written over fifty books on the subject, including the widely acclaimed *Royal Air Force in Action* and *NATO Air Power*.

D0993955

Also by Robert Jackson in Sphere Books:

ACES' TWILIGHT

Robert Jackson

THE FORGOTTEN ACES

SPHERE BOOKS LIMITED

A SPHERE BOOK

First published in Great Britain by
Sphere Books Ltd 1989

ISBN 0 7474 0310 4

Typeset by Selectmove Ltd, London
Reproduced, printed and bound in Great Britain by
BPCC Hazell Books
Aylesbury, Bucks, England
Member of BPCC Ltd.

Sphere Books Ltd
A Division of
Macdonald & Co (Publishers) Ltd
Orbit House
1 New Fetter Lane
London EC4A 1AR
A member of Maxwell Macmillan Pergamon Publishing Corporation

Introduction

The term 'ace', as applied to fighter pilots, originated in France during the 1914–18 War. It was later qualified, by the Americans, to include any pilot who had destroyed five or more enemy aircraft.

During the 1939–45 War, the 'ace factor' was eagerly seized upon by the German and American propaganda machines. Neither the British nor the Japanese recognised it; to this day, the UK Ministry of Defence (RAF) will not admit that any one pilot was the official top-scorer.

Unofficially, the leading RAF 'ace' of World War Two is Group Captain J.E. Johnson, although there is even doubt about that. Johnson scored 38 victories, but this total may have been surpassed by one, and possibly two, other RAF pilots. The top-scoring Allied ace was Colonel Ivan Kozhedub, with 62, while America's Dick Bong had 40 victories.

Germany's leading fighter ace was Major Erich Hartmann, who destroyed an unbelievable 352 aircraft, mostly on the Eastern Front. There is no reason to doubt his claim, nor those of other German fighter pilots who registered phenomenal successes. Apart from the fact that they inflicted terrible losses on the Soviet Air Force following the German invasion of Russia, such men were in action almost continuously from beginning to end; for the *Luftwaffe*'s fighter pilots, there were no rest tours with training schools. Similarly, Japan's leading aces – beginning with

Lieutenant Tetsuzo Iwamoto, 94 victories – fought throughout the Pacific War.

But this book is not about the leading aces, nor about other fighter pilots whose personal charisma or circumstances brought them an undue share of publicity. It is an attempt to follow the course of the air war through the experiences of lesser-known fighter pilots, those who for various reasons never entered the limelight – or, if they did, not until long after the war was over and their exploits became known.

Robert Jackson

CHAPTER ONE

First Encounters

It was the afternoon of 4 September, 1939, and the Second World War was four hours old. On the *Luftwaffe* airfield at Nordholz, guarding the approaches to the big German naval base at Wilhelmshaven, a sudden alert sent the pilots of No 2 Squadron, Fighter Wing 77 – II/JG 77 – racing for their Messerschmitt 109s. RAF bombers were attempting to attack warships moored off Wilhelmshaven, including the battle-cruisers *Scharnhorst* and *Gneisenau*.

Climbing at full throttle over the anchorage, Sergeant Alfred Held sighted a twin-engined bomber heading for the cover of a bank of cloud. It was a Vickers Wellington. Held closed in, braving heavy fire from the Wellington's rear gun turret, and fired at the bomber in short, accurate bursts. The bomber began to stream petrol vapour, which quickly ignited, and went down in flames. Alfred Held's victim, which belonged to No 9 Squadron, RAF Bomber Command, was the first RAF aircraft to fall to a *Luftwaffe* fighter pilot in the Second World War.

On 16 October, it was the *Luftwaffe*'s turn to venture into British territory for the first time. At 13.00 hours, a force of Junkers Ju 88 bombers of No 1 Squadron, Bomber Wing 30 (I/KG 30) took off from Westerland, on the island of Sylt, with orders to attack British warships – primarily the battle-cruiser HMS *Hood* – at Rosyth, in the Firth of Forth. The Ju 88s flew in loose formation as they approached the target

1

area 75 minutes later; German intelligence had indicated that the RAF had only a handful of obsolescent Gloster Gladiator biplane fighters in Scotland. In fact, intelligence was wrong. RAF Fighter Command had two Squadrons of Spitfires, Nos 602 and 603, at Turnhouse near Edinburgh, and that very morning the Hurricanes of No 607 Squadron had flown into Drem, on the southern bank of the Firth.

Sections of both Spitfire squadrons were 'scrambled' to intercept the raiders. The first to make contact with the enemy was Blue Section of No 602 Squadron led by Flight Lieutenant George Pinkerton. Climbing to 10,000 feet with orders to patrol Turnhouse, the pilots sighted nine Ju 88s dive-bombing the warships off Rosyth and gave chase, latching on to the leading bomber as it pulled out of its dive and raced away over the water towards May Island. The Junkers, flown by I/KG 30's commanding officer, Captain Helmut Pohle, was attacked by each of the three Spitfires in turn. The bursts of gunfire killed Pohle's flight engineer and rear gunner and mortally wounded his navigator. First one engine failed as bullets tore into it, then the other. Pohle spotted a trawler and turned towards it, using all his strength to keep the Junkers airborne. Then the bomber ploughed into the sea and he lost consciousness. A few minutes later the trawler crew fished him out of the sinking aircraft and he woke up five days later in Port Edwards hospital. Meanwhile, Red Section of No 603 Squadron, led by Squadron Leader E.H. Stevens, had pursued a twin-engined bomber north of Dalkeith. The aircraft was a Heinkel 111 of KG 26, its task to cause a diversion and also to observe the results of the Ju 88s' attack. Another section of No 603 Squadron, led by Flight Lieutenant Pat Gifford, also joined the chase, and between them they sent the Heinkel down into the sea off Port Seaton. Three crew members were picked up shocked but unhurt; the fourth was dead.

The CO of No 602 Squadron, Squadron Leader Douglas Farquhar, and two of his pilots, Flight Lieutenant A.V.R. 'Sandy' Johnstone and Flying Officer Ferguson, had landed after an earlier and fruitless patrol a few minutes before the enemy bombers appeared over the Firth. They now took off and joined the battle, in time to catch a Ju 88 heading east at 2,000 feet off Aberdour. Joined by two Spitfires of No 603

2

Squadron, they made repeated attacks on the Junkers and sent it down into the sea. None of the crew escaped.

One of the pilots in George Pinkerton's section on this first day of action for Fighter Command was Flying Officer Archie McKellar. A diminutive man, only five feet four inches tall, McKellar was born in Paisley in 1912 and had two childhood ambitions: to become a plasterer and to learn to fly. Overcoming all manner of family objections, he achieved both. In 1936 he joined No 602 (City of Glasgow) Squadron, Auxiliary Air Force – having already gained his pilot's licence at the Scottish Flying Club – and was called up for active service at the outbreak of war.

On 29 November 1939, Red Section of No 602 Squadron, including McKellar, was scrambled to intercept two Heinkels, one circling on reconnaissance over Rosyth, the other over Dalkeith. McKellar, guided by anti-aircraft fire, was the first to sight the second Heinkel, and drew ahead of the rest of his section. Diving into the attack, he opened fire from 200 yards, giving the bomber two bursts. The first struck the Heinkel's wing root and killed its dorsal gunner, the second riddled its tail surfaces. McKellar drew away to make another firing pass, but was beaten to it by three Spitfires of No 603 Squadron, whose fire hit the bomber's starboard wing and cockpit area. The Heinkel crash-landed in a field at Kidlaw, near Haddington, with both gunners dead and the pilot wounded. Only the navigator was unhurt. It was the first enemy aircraft to fall on the British mainland in the 1939–45 War.

Four days before Christmas, McKellar was one of several pilots who were scrambled to intercept a formation of suspect aircraft approaching the Scottish coast. Over the Firth of Forth they sighted six twin-engined bombers with twin tail fins slipping in and out of cloud. Identifying them as Dornier Do 17s, the Spitfire pilots attacked and shot two of them down. But the bombers were not Dorniers: they were Handley Page Hampdens, returning from a raid on Sylt and, because of a bad navigational error, making landfall much too far to the south. They had been heading for RAF Lossiemouth, and had mistaken the Firth of Forth for the Moray Firth. It was not the last time that such a tragedy would occur in the course of the war.

3

Although the two Auxiliary squadrons in Scotland had several skirmishes with the enemy in the winter months of 1939–40, results were mostly inconclusive, but on 13 January 1940, No 602 Squadron, assisted by the Hurricanes of No 111 Squadron from RAF Acklington in Northumberland, shot a Heinkel into the sea off Carnoustie.

The majority of 'kills' so far had been shared between several pilots, although Squadron Leader Farquhar had been given the credit for the Junkers destroyed on 16 October. Farquhar's next chance came on 9 February, 1940, when, accompanied by Flying Officer A.M. Grant on a patrol over the mouth of the Firth of Forth, he was vectored (steered) by ground control to intercept an enemy aircraft some twenty miles out to sea. The enemy turned out to be a Heinkel 111, which dived into cloud as Farquhar attacked. The Spitfire pilot followed into the murk while Grant circled, waiting to catch the Heinkel in case it feinted back, but Farquhar caught up with it in a clear patch and opened fire, hitting it in one engine. The Heinkel turned in towards the coast and made a wheels-up landing near North Berwick. Three of its crew escaped unhurt, but Farquhar's machine-gun fire had seriously wounded the dorsal gunner, who died later in hospital.

Farquhar was in action again on 22 February. Together with Flying Officer George Proudman, he attacked a Heinkel 111 at 11.50 hours, his fire wounding the German dorsal gunner in both legs and putting the bomber's engines out of action. The enemy pilot turned in over the coast and made a skilful crash-landing at Coldinham, near St Abbs Head in Berwickshire. Farquhar, circling overhead, saw the crew scramble clear, assisting the injured gunner, and realised that they were about to set fire to their more or less intact aircraft, so he decided to land alongside and stop them. Unfortunately, the Spitfire hit a patch of mud as it rolled down the field and turned over on its back.

Farquhar was unhurt, but hung helplessly upside down in his straps until the Heinkel's crew, seeing his predicament, ran across and helped him out of it – having first set light to the nose section of their bomber. Farquhar, seeing some armed Home Guard volunteers approaching, advised the German crew to surrender to him, which they did. Farquhar collected their Luger pistols, and was promptly arrested by the Home Guard, who took him for one of the enemy. He extricated himself from this fresh embarrassment by delving into his pocket and producing an Inland Revenue tax return form, which he had received that morning!

On 13 March 1940, Farquhar, with three victories to his credit, was promoted to wing commander and given command of RAF Martlesham Heath in Suffolk, a fighter station. He continued to fly in combat occasionally, and in November 1940, at the tail-end of the Battle of Britain, he shared in the destruction of two Junkers Ju 87 Stukas. Later in the war, he became Wing Leader of the Hornchurch Wing, flying a number of fighter sweeps over occupied France.

Few of the pilots who fought those early skirmishes with the *Luftwaffe* went on to become aces by destroying five or more enemy aircraft. For example, of 39 pilots who fought with No 602 Squadron during the Battle of Britain, from July to October 1940, thirteen were killed or injured, and seven more lost their lives in the war.

There were, of course, exceptions. Flight Lieutenant Robert Findlay Boyd, one of the 'original' auxiliaries, ended his war in the Far East with twelve victories, some of them Japanese, and retired as a group captain with a DSO, DFC and Bar; another 'original', Sergeant Andrew McDowall, later became a wing commander with at least nine victories; and Sandy Johnstone, later to become an air vice-marshal, shot down at least six enemy aircraft.

But the most notable exception was Archie McKellar. In June 1940, McKellar was promoted to flight lieutenant and posted to command a flight of No 605 Squadron, which was flying Hurricanes from Drem. On 15 August, with the *Luftwaffe* pounding RAF airfields in southern England in the opening phase of what was to become known as the Battle of Britain, 63 Heinkel 111s took off from bases in Norway to attack airfields in the north of England. The bombers were escorted by 26 Messerschmitt 110s. The fighters would be operating at the limit of their range, but the Germans did not expect serious trouble; according to *Luftwaffe* intelligence, most of the RAF's northern fighter squadrons had been transferred south, to help counter the heavy air attacks in No 11 Group's area. Once again, however, the German intelligence was at fault. Unknown to the incoming

Heinkels and Messerschmitts, five squadrons of Spitfires and Hurricanes lay in their path. One of them was No 605 Squadron.

At 1300 hours, the Messerschmitts, sweeping ahead of the bombers, were heavily engaged over the Farne Islands by the Spitfires of No 72 Squadron and the Hurricanes of No 79, both from RAF Acklington in Northumberland. When the pilots of No 605 Squadron sighted the Heinkels approaching the River Tyne from the north-east, they consequently found that the bomber formation was unescorted.

McKellar's 'B' Flight was the first to make contact with the Heinkels, which were flying in groups of 20–25, straggling back across the sky for several miles. McKellar ordered his pilots into line astern and told them to follow him into the sun. Then he led them in a diving attack on the rear aircraft of the leading group. Lining up on a Heinkel, he opened fire from 250 yards. After one three-second burst the bomber fell away in a spiral dive and McKellar was forced to break away sharply as he came under fire from a pair of Heinkels behind him. 'We were by then over Newcastle,' he wrote later in his combat report, 'and I ordered my flight to make individual attacks as I considered harrying tactics were the best way of defeating the object of bombing Tyneside.'

Some of the bombers, in fact, jettisoned their loads over the Tyne shipyards and veered away out to sea. The remainder flew on towards Sunderland, still harried by No 605 Squadron. Archie McKellar attacked another Heinkel, which took violent evasive action and got away, then he selected the leading bomber in the formation and swept down in a beam attack, giving the aircraft a long eight-second burst. It started to go down, with both engines pouring smoke. McKellar turned steeply and fired at a Heinkel which flashed across his nose; that, too, began to burn. Looking round, he picked up a straggler and closed in astern, firing off the remainder of his ammunition. He saw the bomber's dorsal gunner suddenly throw up his hands and disappear beneath his cupola; an instant later the Heinkel's starboard engine began to trail grey smoke. Low on fuel, and with ammunition exhausted, McKellar left the bomber to its uncertain fate and headed for the nearest airfield.

During the engagement over the Tyne, the pilots of No 605 Squadron destroyed four enemy aircraft and damaged six more.

The remainder, under attack now by the Spitfires of No 41 Squadron from RAF Catterick and the Hurricanes of No 607 Squadron from RAF Usworth, near Sunderland, unloaded their bombs more or less at random and made their escape as quickly as possible. Behind them, scattered along the coast, they left the wrecks of eight Heinkels and six Me 110s. It was a high price to pay for failure.

McKellar did not get into the thick of fighting until 7 September 1940 – the day the *Luftwaffe* switched its main attacks from the hard-hit RAF fighter airfields to London, a decision that was to have a profound influence on the outcome of the battle – when No 605 Squadron moved to Croydon. On the following day McKellar's flight destroyed five enemy aircraft in a single engagement, although he did not score personally, but on 9 September he achieved an amazing quadruple success when his flight engaged a formation of Heinkel 111s and Messerschmitt 109s over Maidstone.

The Hurricanes attacked the Messerschmitts first, and McKellar destroyed one with a three-second burst. He then turned to make a head-on attack on three Heinkels which were flying in line abreast, close together. He opened fire on the centre bomber at 700 yards and kept firing as the distance narrowed. The bomber's wings burst into flames and McKellar switched his fire to the left-hand Heinkel. At that moment the centre bomber blew up, the explosion destroying the right-hand aircraft too. An instant later the one on the left lost a wing and also went spiralling earthwards.

There seemed to be no holding McKellar after that. From 9 September he averaged a victory a day for eight days, his victims including He 111s, Me 109s and a Dornier 17. On 16 September he made a lone night sortie, found a Heinkel 111 trapped in searchlights and shot it down.

His most successful day was on 15 October. That afternoon, he was patrolling with No 605 Squadron – he was now its commanding officer – when the Hurricanes encountered fifteen Me 109s, with 40 or 50 above and behind, in the Sevenoaks area. McKellar's combat report tells what happened.

'I attacked the Number One and saw a bomb being dropped from this machine. I fired and pieces fell off his wing and dense white smoke and vapour came from him and he went into a violent outside spin. In my mirror I could see another 109 coming to attack me and therefore turned sharply right and found myself just below and behind another 109. I opened fire and saw my De Wilde [explosive ammunition] hitting his machine. It burst into flames and went down inverted east of Biggin Hill. As I again had a 109 on my tail I spiralled down to 15,000 feet and by this time there appeared to be 109s straggling all over the sky. I followed one, pulled my boost control and made up on him. I gave a burst from dead astern and at once his radiator appeared to be hit as dense white vapour came back at me and my windscreen fogged up. This speedily cleared and I gave another burst and this machine burst into flames and fell into a wood with a quarry near it, west of Maidstone.'

A minute later McKellar sighted yet another 109, slipping in and out of cloud. Still using boost, he overhauled it rapidly and it caught fire after a stern attack, the pilot baling out. Two hours later, in the course of another sortie, McKellar destroyed another 109 to make five in one day.

By the end of October, Archie McKellar had been officially credited with the destruction of twenty enemy aircraft. On 1 November, he took off in his Hurricane at 07.40 hours and never came back. No one knows exactly what happened; his aircraft was seen to fall from a high level and then fly inverted around a country mansion before crashing in the grounds. An Me 109 was also shot down during the morning patrol, and since no other 605 Squadron pilot claimed it, it could have been McKellar's last victim.

Archie McKellar's meteoric rise to fame had taken only seven weeks. In that time he had been awarded DSO, DFC and Bar, but so hectic had been the fighting over southern England that there had been no time for him to collect the medals. It was his father who, proudly if sorrowfully, received them from King George VI.

While Archie McKellar and his fellow Auxiliary Air Force pilots were skirmishing with the *Luftwaffe* over Scotland in the closing weeks of 1939, the German fighter pilots were reaping their own harvest against RAF Bomber Command on the other side of the North Sea. On 3 December, 24 Vickers Wellington bombers of Nos 38, 115 and 149 Squadrons took off from their bases at Marham and Mildenhall to attack German warships off

Heligoland in daylight. The Wellingtons ran through heavy anti-aircraft fire as they made their approach and two of them were hit, though not seriously. A few moments later the bombers were attacked from astern by Messerschmitt 109s and 110s. These attacks were ineffective and at least one of the fighters was damaged. The Wellingtons bombed from 8,000 feet, but although some of their bombs fell in the target area no hits were registered on the warships. All the aircraft returned safely to base.

This operation seemed to justify the belief that a tight bomber formation was sufficient defence against fighter attacks in daylight. The Messerschmitt pilots had seemed wary of facing the Wellingtons' rear armament of four .303 machine-guns at a range closer than 400 yards, and although one straggling bomber had been attacked simultaneously by four fighters it had fought its way clear without having sustained a single hit. Bomber Command was sufficiently encouraged by the result of the 3 December raid to try again.

The opportunity came on 14 December, when it was reported that the cruisers *Nürnberg* and *Leipzig* had been torpedoed by a British submarine and were limping back to the Jade Estuary, badly damaged. Twelve Wellingtons of No 99 Squadron set out from Newmarket to attack them. The weather was bad, and by the time the Dutch coast was sighted the Wellingtons were forced to fly at 600 feet or less in order to stay below the overcast. The pilots had been ordered not to attack unless they could bomb from at least 2,000 feet; they nevertheless continued on course in the hope that the cloud would lift.

By this time they were coming under heavy and continuous fire from warships and armed merchantmen lying in the approaches to the estuary. At this low altitude the bombers presented excellent targets and several were hit. Suddenly, the flak died away as enemy fighters came speeding up. They were the Messerschmitt 109s of II/JG 27, led by Major Harry von Bülow, and this time the pilots showed no hesitation in pressing home their attacks to point-blank range. The Wellingtons' gunners accounted for one Me 109, which was seen to crash in flames, but the fighter destroyed five bombers in a matter of minutes. A sixth Wellington crashed on landing at Newmarket.

Despite the unfortunate outcome of this raid, another attack on the German Fleet was planned for 18 December. Twenty-four

Wellingtons of Nos 9, 37 and 149 Squadrons, loaded with 500-lb semi-armour-piercing bombs, set out to attack any shipping located in the Schillig Roads, Wilhelmshaven or the Jade Estuary. The minimum bombing altitude was to be 10,000 feet.

About two-thirds of the way over the North Sea, two aircraft dropped out with engine trouble. The remainder pressed on in brilliant, cloudless weather, making a detour around Heligoland to avoid the anti-aircraft batteries there and turning in towards Wilhelmshaven from the north.

The first German fighters to intercept the bomber force were six Messerschmitt 109s of 10/JG 26 from Jever, led by First Lieutenant Johannes 'Macki' Steinhoff. The 26-year-old pilot had originally joined the German Navy in 1934, but had transferred to the *Luftwaffe* in 1936. His leadership talents were such that, only three years later, he had risen to the command of JG 26's 10th Group.

Steinhoff and his wingman, Corporal Hailmayr, each made two beam attacks on individual Wellingtons. Both bombers fell in flames. For 'Macki' Steinhoff, it was the first success on a road that would end, 167 victories and five and a half years later, in the blazing wreckage of a Messerschmitt 262 jet fighter – an accident he would remarkably survive, although at the cost of terrible disfigurement.

After their first kills, the Me 109s sheered off as the bombers flew at 13,000 feet through the heavy flak of the Wilhelmshaven defences. The Wellingtons crossed the naval base without dropping any bombs, then turned and crossed it again, still without bombing, before heading away towards the north-west. By this time, the Me 109s of 10/JG 26 had been joined by the twin-engined Me 110s of ZG 76 and the 109s of JG 77, and the combined force of fighters now fell on the Wellington formation as it passed to the north of the island of Wangerooge.

One of the pilots who entered the battle at this juncture was Lieutenant Helmut Lent, flying an Me 110 of ZG 76. Sighting a pair of Wellingtons near Borkum Island, he attacked from the beam and then astern, his fire killing the rear gunner. With the latter dead the bomber was defenceless against attacks from behind, and Lent continued to fire at it from close range until its engines began to stream smoke. It crash-landed on Borkum, and only one of its six-man crew got out alive. Lent went after the other bomber and made a determined attack on it, again from astern. Both its engines caught fire and it went down, breaking up on impact with the sea. Like Steinhoff, Helmut Lent had begun to climb a ladder of fame which would bring him 110 victories, mostly against the RAF's night bombers.

On this grim December day twelve Wellingtons failed to return, an appalling loss that highlighted the folly of sending bombers deep into enemy territory in broad daylight without fighter escort. After December 1939, RAF Bomber Command's policy was to operate increasingly under cover of darkness, while later in the war the Americans were to adhere to the theory that bomber formations with heavy defensive armament were capable of making successful daylight penetration attacks. They, too, would learn the hard way.

The consequences of sending unescorted bombers on daylight missions into enemy territory had also been brought home to the RAF in France, where Fairey Battle light bombers engaged in this kind of activity had suffered terrible losses. On 20 September 1939, for example, two out of three Battles of No 88 Squadron were shot down by Me 109s over Aachen. Then, on the last day of the month, five Battles of No 150 Squadron were sent out to make a reconnaissance of the Saarbrücken area. They had just penetrated enemy territory when they were attacked by eight Me 109s, and four of the Battles were shot down in as many minutes. After that, the Battles serving with RAF's Advanced Air Striking Force in France were withdrawn from daylight operations.

For the aircrews who faced each other on the Western Front in that autumn and winter of 1939, the term 'Phoney War' was a misnomer. From the very first week of the war, Allied and German fighters skirmished over the Maginot Line on an almost daily basis, except when the state of the weather precluded such meetings, and each side did its best to shoot down the other's reconnaissance aircraft.

The two fighter squadrons deployed to France in support of the Advanced Air Striking Force were Nos 1 and 73, both operating Hawker Hurricanes. No 1 Squadron was based at Vassincourt, and when a Dornier 17 reconnaissance aircraft flew directly over the airfield on 30 October 1939 it was intercepted and destroyed near Sauvigny by Pilot Officer P.W.O. 'Boy' Mould, who thus became the first RAF fighter pilot to destroy

11

an enemy aircraft on the Continent in World War Two. (The first enemy aircraft to be destroyed by the RAF over France in WW2 was actually claimed by Sergeant F. Letchford, the rear gunner of a Fairey Battle – the sole survivor of the three attacked by Me 109s over Aachen on 20 September.) Mould was later to lose his life on 1 October 1941, while commanding No 185 Squadron in Malta. His Hurricane was hit by an Italian Macchi C.202 fighter; Mould baled out and came down in the sea, but he was never found.

No 73 Squadron, at Norrent-Fontes, scored its first victory on 8 November 1939. At 10.00 that morning, after a fifteen-minute battle that ended in a screaming dive from 26,000 feet to ground level, a Hurricane pilot watched the Dornier 17 he had been chasing dive into the ground and explode. The pilot was a young New Zealand flying officer named James Edgar Kain – 'Cobber' Kain, whose personality and prowess in the cockpit of a fighter were to capture the imagination of the British and French public during the months to come.

Kain, who was 21 when war broke out, had joined the RAF in 1937. He had already learned to fly in New Zealand. He gained his second victory – another Dornier 17 – on 23 November 1939, just before the onset of bad weather severely curtailed flying in France for several weeks. It was 3 March 1940 before he once more got to serious grips with the enemy.

At 13.00 that day, Kain and a sergeant pilot were patrolling the front line at 20,000 feet, after escorting a French Potez 63 reconnaissance aircraft, when they sighted anti-aircraft bursts over Thionville and flew towards them.

A minute later, Kain spotted seven Heinkel 111s some 5,000 feet higher up and at once gave chase, gradually leaving the other Hurricane behind. Suddenly, as he gained on the Heinkels, Kain heard a warning shout from his number two; they were being shadowed by six Me 109s. Kain looked round, just in time to see a 109 open fire on him. Cannon shells struck the Hurricane's fuselage and then the 109 was passed and diving away. Almost at once Kain was attacked by a second 109, which also scored hits on his aircraft. This time, Kain was ready for the enemy fighter as it overshot; three short bursts and the Messerschmitt went down, trailing black smoke. Kain, who by this time was well inside Germany, began a turn towards the Allied lines, only to be hit by a third Messerschmitt. The Hurricane's engine stopped with a loud bang and smoke filled the cockpit. Unable to see his compass, Kain pointed the nose of his aircraft in what he hoped was the direction of Metz and trimmed the aircraft for a long glide, turning his oxygen full on in order to breathe. A few minutes later, by which time flames were breaking through into the cockpit, he crossed the front line and made a perfect emergency landing on a French airfield.

Kain was awarded the DFC for this action. A few days later he brought his score to five enemy aircraft destroyed, so becoming the first RAF 'ace' of World War Two. His victories mounted rapidly after the German offensive in the West began on 10 May 1940, by 27 May his total of confirmed kills had risen to seventeen. He was awarded a Bar to his DFC, and then No 73 Squadron was ordered back to England. On 6 June, Kain took off from the squadron's airfield at Echmines and, as a farewell gesture, launched into an impromptu aerobatic routine. Eye-witnesses saw his Hurricane enter a series of rapid flick-rolls to the left, then it suddenly lost flying speed and went into a spin. There was insufficient height for the pilot to recover, and the Hurricane hit the ground and burst into flames. Kain was thrown from the cockpit, and died instantly from head injuries.

Kain's closest rival in France during the so-called 'Phoney War' was Flying Officer Leslie R. Clisby, an Australian who had started his Service career as a cadet in the RAAF and who had come to England on a short-service commission in 1937. Clisby was credited with six victories while flying with No 1 Squadron up to the end of April 1940; three of them – all Me 109s – were destroyed on two consecutive days in that month. He destroyed eight more during the first four days of May, bringing his score to fourteen. He shot down three Me 109s in a furious battle on 11 May, then the rudder of his Hurricane was partially shot away by another enemy fighter. Barely able to control the aircraft, he headed earthwards to make a forced landing. Suddenly, he saw a Heinkel 111 below and ahead of him. Manoeuvring his Hurricane cautiously, he fired a burst into the German bomber, which crash-landed. Clisby landed nearby, drew his revolver as he jumped from the cockpit, and chased the German crew over the fields, firing as he gained on them. The Germans stopped, raised their hands, and the Australian took them prisoner, handing them over to the French authorities in a nearby village before returning to his squadron.

Three days later, Leslie Clisby's Hurricane was seen going down in flames near Reims. He was never heard of again.

The 'Phoney War' period also witnessed the rise of Germany's leading air aces, many of whom had fought during the Spanish Civil War, where they had scored their early victories. Some had added to their scores during the brief campaign in Poland in the summer of 1939. The highest-scoring German pilot of the Polish campaign, and the first German ace of World War Two, was Hauptmann Hannes Gentzen, who scored seven victories in an Me 109; but one pilot had already gained twice that many kills during the bitter air fighting in Spain.

His name was Werner Mölders, who in Spain had commanded the 3rd Squadron of *Jagdgruppe* J.88 (III/J.88). In July 1938 this unit received its first Messerschmitt Me 109C-1 fighters, and it was while flying one of these aircraft that Mölders fought his first air combat. While carrying out a patrol over the Northern Front, the pilots of III/J.88 encountered a strong formation of Russian-built I-16 fighters. Mölders soon got on the tail of one of them, but he was over-excited and opened fire when the range was still much too great. The I-16 escaped, but a few seconds later Mölders attacked another. This time there was no mistake; the enemy fighter burst into flames and crashed after Mölders opened fire at point-blank range.

By the time Mölders' tour of duty ended in Spain in October 1938 he had destroyed fourteen enemy aircraft, making him the top-scoring German pilot in the Civil War. More important than that was the experience he had gained in the science of air fighting, experience that was put to good use on his return to Germany. Together with other leading German pilots who had served in Spain, Mölders virtually re-wrote the *Luftwaffe*'s manual of fighter tactics, helping to devise the combat formations which, a few months later, were to prove far superior to any employed by the German Air Force's opponents.

The outbreak of World War Two in September 1939 found Mölders in command of I/JG 53, and it was not long before the unit was in action. On 20 September, after some cautious initial sparring, the *Luftwaffe* and the French Air Force joined battle in earnest over the Franco-German border. During the afternoon, six Curtiss Hawks of the French Groupe de Chasse GC II/5 were escorting a reconnaissance aircraft over the front when the top flight of three French fighters was attacked by four Me 109s, led by Mölders. The Frenchmen broke wildly but they were too late; Mölders got on the tail of a Curtiss and sent it down on fire with a short burst. The pilot baled out. In the air battle that followed a second Curtiss went down, while the French pilots accounted for a 109.

The next day, three Messerschmitts led by Mölders pounced on a luckless French Potez reconnaissance aircraft over Altheim. A very gallant French pilot in a Morane 406 fighter came to the Potez' rescue, but he was too late and the Messerschmitts attacked him in turn. Mölders allowed his wingmen to get in the first bursts, then he closed in and gave the Morane the coup de grâce from point-blank range. The French pilot baled out, but his parachute failed to open.

The fighter pilots of JG 53 saw frequent action during the winter of 1939–40, and in the spring of 1940, with the air battles flaring up with renewed violence, Mölders gained additional victories. By 10 May, his personal score stood at 25 enemy aircraft destroyed.

On that day, preceded by massive air attacks, the German Panzer divisions struck westwards across the River Meuse. But before the *Bliztkrieg* in France was over, RAF fighter pilots would have fought a desperate, heroic and hopeless campaign far to the north, in Norway.

CHAPTER TWO

The Gladiators

On 9 April 1940 – the day that German forces landed in Norway by sea and air – the tiny Royal Norwegian Air Force possessed only one fighter squadron. Based at Fornebu airfield, and charged with the defence of Oslo, it was equipped with nine Gloster Gladiators, biplane fighters supplied by Britain a couple of years earlier. The handful of Norwegian pilots fought valiantly and succeeded in destroying a number of enemy aircraft; apart from one pilot who was badly wounded, the rest survived the encounters and would have gone on fighting to the last, had not their airfields and aircraft been destroyed by German bombing.

In RAF service, the Gladiator had been mostly replaced – except overseas – by modern fighter types such as the Hurricane and Spitfire. However, one unit of RAF Fighter Command – No 263 Squadron – was still using it, and on 24 April 1940 eighteen Gladiators of this squadron flew from the aircraft carrier HMS *Glorious* to land on the frozen surface of Lake Lesjaskogen. This was about 40 miles from Andalsnes, where a British infantry brigade had landed five days earlier. A second British brigade and three battalions of French Chasseurs had also been landed at Namsos, farther north, the idea being that these forces would advance jointly to recapture the German-held port of Trondheim. The Gladiators were to provide the necessary fighter support.

Conditions at Lesjaskogen were appalling. Working in sub-zero temperatures, a handful of airmen worked all night to refuel and arm the Gladiators; even then, when they checked the aircraft at daybreak they found that the carburettors and control surfaces were frozen solid. Two Gladiators were made airworthy by 05.00, and these took off to patrol the lake. They had not been airborne long when their pilots sighted a Heinkel 115 reconnaissance seaplane, which they attacked and shot down. Under cover of the diversion, a Heinkel 111 flew across the lake unopposed and dropped a stick of bombs, but without doing any damage.

The Gladiators flew in support of the ground forces throughout the morning of 26 April, often taking off while the lake was under attack. No 263 Squadron suffered its first loss at 11.00 when a Gladiator was destroyed on the ground by a low-flying Heinkel; its pilot, Sergeant Forrest, had just stepped clear of his aircraft. In the space of an hour, nine more Gladiators were destroyed, all on the ground, in exchange for one Heinkel 111 shot down by Flight Lieutenant Mills. At noon, an intruding Heinkel 111 was attacked by a section of Gladiators led by Pilot Officer McNamara; the bomber went into a spin and crashed on the edge of the lake.

Early in the afternoon, the surviving Gladiators shot down another Heinkel and badly damaged its companion, which limped away trailing smoke. Not long afterwards, Squadron Leader J.W. Donaldson and Flight Lieutenant Mills caught a Heinkel near Andalsnes and shot it down into a ravine. That evening, Mills became involved in a running fight with half a dozen Junkers 88s. His ammunition ran out, followed by his fuel, and he had to make a forced landing. He had just finished surveying the bullet holes in the battle-worn Gladiator's fuselage and wings when two Heinkels roared overhead and destroyed it with machine-gun fire.

When darkness fell, the surface of Lake Lesjaskogen was pitted and torn by countless bomb craters. Only four Gladiators were left now, and these were evacuated to Andalsnes. This small force was further depleted on the morning of 27 April, when Pilot Officer Craig-Adams took off on a reconnaissance sortie. He had been flying for about ten minutes when the Gladiator's worn-out Mercury engine seized up. The pilot baled out and made his way safely back to Andalsnes.

It was the end. Later in the day the last fuel stocks ran out, and the next day the squadron personnel received orders to destroy their remaining aircraft. That evening they embarked on the cargo vessel *Delius,* and after running the gauntlet of several dive-bombing attacks off the Norwegian coast, they reached Scapa Flow naval base on 1 May without further incident.

On 14 May, No 263 Squadron, now re-equipped with Gladiator Mk IIs, once more sailed for Norway aboard HMS *Glorious.* This time, the aircraft were to fly from the carrier to a landing ground at Bardufoss, near Narvik, from where they were to provide air support for the Allied forces' second Norwegian Expedition. It was 21 May before the carrier reached her flying-off station, and the first two sections of Gladiators, each led by a Fairey Swordfish of the Fleet Air Arm, took off from her flight deck in sleet. With the weather deteriorating, one section returned to the carrier and landed-on safely; the other, lost in fog and snow, crashed headlong into a mountainside at Soreisa. The Swordfish crew was killed, as was one of the Gladiator pilots, Pilot Officer Richards; the other, Flight Lieutenant Mills, was badly injured.

An advance force of eight Gladiators eventually reached Bardufoss on 22 May, and went into action immediately. On that day, No 263 Squadron suffered its first aircrew loss in action when Pilot Officer Craig-Adams failed to return; his body was later found in the wreckage of his aircraft, which lay close to that of a Heinkel 111. The opinion was that the two had collided in the course of an air combat. The remaining Gladiators flew in the next day, making a total of fourteen airworthy aircraft, and soon after their arrival Sergeant Whall shot down a Heinkel 111; however, his own aircraft ran out of fuel and he was forced to bale out.

On the morning of 24 April, four Messerschmitt 110s strafed the squadron's airfield. They were met with highly accurate anti-aircraft fire, and after making a couple of firing passes they drew off to a safe distance and circled watchfully. Pilot Officer Grant-Ede took off and attacked the enemy formation single-handed, and after a brief exchange of fire the Messerschmitts dived away and disappeared.

Grant-Ede was airborne again that afternoon. With Flying Officer Riley, he came upon a lone Heinkel 111 flying at 500 feet over Bardufoss. He fired a burst from close astern, killing the rear gunner, then half-rolled away. Riley attacked in turn, putting the Heinkel's starboard engine out of action, then a third Gladiator, flown by Flight Lieutenant C.B. Hull, dropped into the fight and riddled the bomber's port motor. The bomber slewed round in a diving turn and crash-landed near Salanger, its crew being taken prisoner.

The next day, while on patrol, Grant-Ede encountered a big four-engined Junkers Ju 90 transport at 15,000 feet north of Harstadt. He closed in, firing two bursts at short range, and the aircraft went down into the sea off Dyroy Island. Grant-Ede caught a second Ju 90 on a subsequent sortie, killing the transport's rear gunner and putting all four of its engines out of action with accurate bursts of fire from close range; the aircraft crashed in flames on Finnoen Island, south of Narvik. A third Ju 90 was shot down that evening near Harstadt by Pilot Officer Purdy and Sergeant Kitchener.

The next day, 26 June, saw No 263 Squadron engaged in some bitter air fighting. During one of the first sorties of the day, Flight Lieutenant Williams and Sergeant Milligan destroyed a Junkers 88 over Skaanland, and a little later in the day a section of three Gladiators, flown by Flight Lieutenant Hull, Lieutenant Lydekker, RN, and Pilot Officer Falkson deployed to the airstrip at Bodo, close to the front line. Soon after their arrival, Hull attacked a Heinkel 111 over Saltefjord and set one of its engines on fire, and immediately afterwards he sighted a Junkers Ju 52 transport flying in formation with another Heinkel. The latter turned away, and Hull shot the Junkers down in flames.

Hull turned to intercept two more Heinkels, which eluded him, but then he sighted a pair of Ju 52s heading for a cloud bank. He attacked one of them, using the last of the ammunition in his wing guns, and shot it down. Almost at once, he sighted another He 111 below him and dived to attack it; only his nose machine-gun was working, but he succeeded in damaging the enemy bomber, which departed with smoke trailing from one engine. Hull had barely sufficient fuel to regain Bodo, where he landed at dusk.

Meanwhile, back at Bardufoss, it had been a hectic day for the rest of No 263 Squadron. Some vicious fighting had taken place over Harstadt when Pilot Officers Purdy and Bentley attacked six Dornier 17s and shot down one each, subsequently driving off the others. On a later patrol over Harstadt, Flying Officer Riley and Pilot Officer Parnall came upon a formation of Heinkel 111s which they attacked. Two Heinkels went down in flames, but Riley was wounded in the neck and hands.

On this day, the Gladiators were joined at Bardufoss by fifteen Hawker Hurricanes of No 46 Squadron. These aircraft had, in fact, accompanied No 263 Squadron on its first expedition to Norway aboard HMS *Glorious*, but had been unable to fly off because their intended landing ground at Skaanland had not been ready. Eighteen Hurricanes were actually flown off the carrier on 26 May, with Skaanland as their destination, but the first three to land nosed over in soft ground and so the rest were diverted to Bardufoss. The Hurricanes scored their first success on 28 May, when Pilot Officer McGregor destroyed a Ju 88 over Tjelbotn, and later that day a section of Hurricanes surprised two Dornier Do 26 seaplanes on the water at Rombaksfjord, disembarking troops, and destroyed both of them.

Meanwhile, on 27 May, Bodo airstrip and the adjacent town had been heavily bombed and strafed by Ju 87 Stukas and Messerschmitt 110s. Hull and Lydekker took off to intercept, each shooting down a Ju 87, but Hull was attacked by an Me 110 and forced down in the hills, wounded in the head and knee by cannon shell splinters. He was evacuated to England two days later. Lydekker was also wounded in the neck and shoulder, and – unable to land at Bodo because of the prowling Messerschmitts – he flew his aircraft to Bardufoss, where he crash-landed.

The *Luftwaffe* made few sorties into No 263 Squadron's sector during the next five days, and the exhausted pilots and ground crews were able to snatch a few hours' well-earned rest. The only successful combat took place on 28 May, when Flight Lieutenant Williams caught a Heinkel 111 attacking shipping in Ofotfjord and drove it off with both engines pouring smoke. During this week of comparative respite, the squadron flew about 30 sorties against ground targets, one of which was the German Army Headquarters at Hundalen.

The end in Norway, however, was fast approaching. On 2 June, General Claude Auchinleck, commanding the Allied Expeditionary Force, gave orders for evacuation and, as soon as its reconnaissance aircraft detected what was happening, the *Luftwaffe* renewed its heavy air attacks on both shipping and ground forces in the area of Narvik, the principal port of evacuation. Narvik was to have been covered by the Hurricanes of No 46 Squadron, but owing to the unserviceability of Skaanland, the pilots found themselves at a grave disadvantage, for Bardufoss was a considerable distance away and the time that could be spent over Narvik was consequently short. Nevertheless, the pilots of No 46 Squadron did what they could, destroying or driving off several enemy aircraft as the evacuation got under way, and so did No 263 Squadron. Between dawn and dusk on 2 June the Gladiators flew 55 sorties, and the day saw some magnificent air battles. One of the pilots involved was Pilot Officer L.R. Jacobsen, a 25-year-old New Zealander from Wellington who had joined the RAF in 1938. During the First Norwegian Expedition he had twice engaged enemy aircraft, being credited with one He 111 destroyed and another damaged.

Now, on 2 June, Jacobsen took off with Pilot Officer Wilkie to patrol the area between Narvik and the Swedish border. At 14.45 they encountered two Junkers 88s, and Jacobsen made a beam attack on the leader while Wilkie went after the second Junkers. As Wilkie closed in, his Gladiator was hit by fire from the Ju 88's rear gunner and spun down to crash. The Junkers escaped into a bank of cloud across the Swedish border.

Meanwhile, Jacobsen had opened fire on the leading Junkers from 300 yards, but the German pilot opened his throttles and the fast twin-engined bomber quickly outpaced the Gladiator. Jacobsen chased it into Swedish airspace and fired again from 400 yards, without seeing any result. At that moment the second Junkers re-appeared from cloud cover, passing directly in front of Jacobsen's fighter. He opened fire and hit the enemy aircraft, which went into an apparently uncontrolled dive. As the Junkers was flying at only 300 feet, and the terrain below was stiff with mountains, it was unlikely that the German would have been able to pull out.

Jacobsen himself narrowly avoided the mountain peaks. Climbing at full throttle, he turned back into Norway, and soon afterwards he encountered a mixed formation of He 111s and Ju 88s flying at low level. He turned behind a Heinkel and fired a burst into its forward fuselage; the pilot must have been hit, as the bomber suddenly reared up, stalled, flicked over on its wingtip and blew up on the ground near Bjornfjell. Immediately afterwards, Jacobsen was subjected to a head-on attack by three He 111s and a Ju 88. The New Zealander took evasive action and turned in behind one of the Heinkels, firing a three-second burst into it. Another Heinkel attacked him head-on and he fired a three-second burst into this bomber too before he was forced to break away. The bomber went down in a spiral dive, apparently out of control.

Jacobsen now found himself inside a circle of six He 111s and two Ju 88s which attacked him from above, below and head-on, firing at him with their nose guns. Jacobsen was now fighting for his life. One of the Gladiator's bracing wires was shot away and its engine was hit. Oil sprayed over the windscreen, and through it Jacobsen saw the vague outline of a Heinkel. He fired, and the bomber glided earthwards with both engines stopped.

His ammunition exhausted, Jacobsen managed to evade his attackers and limp back to base. Later, the wreckage of three Heinkels was found just inside the Swedish border, and it was learned that two Ju 88s had also crashed in that area. As Jacobsen was the only pilot to have engaged Junkers 88s on 2 June – apart from the unfortunate Wilkie – the probability is that they were his victims, together with the three Heinkels. Taking the New Zealander's He 111 kill earlier in the campaign into account, this would give him six victories, and so make him the only pilot to become an ace in Norway.

Another pilot who had success on 2 June was Sergeant H.H. Kitchener. His own combat report tells the story.

'I took off in Gladiator N5905 to patrol Narvik district. After being airborne I observed four He 111s in formation 2,000 feet above me. After about three minutes, with F/Lt Williams, I attacked the formation. The He 111s proceeded to dive. Between us we caught up the straggling Heinkel. I attacked from the beam, F/Lt Williams from astern. Both engines and the fuselage caught alight and the aircraft dived out of control and crashed. We then caught up the next straggler and a similar attack was carried out. Both engines caught alight and it subsequently crashed. Both these aircraft can be found between five and twenty miles respectively NE of Narvik.

'For the next twenty minutes, between the two of us we carried out seven more attacks of a similar nature. Both engines of the third Heinkel in formation were put out of action and it was seen to be diving out of control to the ground. We then both attacked a Ju 87; it was one of two and had a large extra tank beneath each side of the mainplanes about four feet from the wing tip. This aircraft put up strong resistance, but the port tank caught alight and the aircraft crashed into the top of a hill some 30 miles south of Narvik. I observed F/Lt Williams closing on a He 111 which was bobbing in and out of clouds. I was unable to catch up at the time, as while I was getting into position a Ju 87 crossed my sights and therefore I attacked. When I had finished it a white stream of smoke was coming from the engine and I lost it in cloud. Further attacks were made but no definite results can be claimed. I returned to base having run out of ammunition.'

Kitchener's description of the Ju 87 shot down by himself and Williams is interesting. The only Stuka unit to operate in Norway, I/St.G 1, was equipped with a long-range version of the dive-bomber, the Ju 87R, which carried long-range tanks under its wings. There can be no doubt about the RAF pilots' victory, but oddly enough *Luftwaffe* records admitted no Stuka losses on 2 June in Norway.

Later in the war, Kitchener flew Westland Whirlwind fighter-bombers on offensive sweeps over France and the Low Countries. In March 1941, he destroyed a Junkers 88, but was hit by return fire and crashed on returning to base. He survived the war and left the RAF in 1946, having reached the rank of wing commander.

Kitchener was lucky. On 7 June, when the collapse came in Norway and the final evacuation took place, the pilots of No 263 Squadron – together with those of No 46 Squadron – were ordered to fly their remaining Gladiators and Hurricanes to the carrier HMS *Glorious*. As No 263 Squadron had more pilots than aircraft, two stayed behind to be evacuated by destroyer. Kitchener was one of them.

All the aircraft landed safely on the carrier, which set course for Scapa Flow. In the afternoon of 8 June 1940, *Glorious* was caught in the open sea by the German battle-cruisers *Scharnhorst* and *Gneisenau*. In a one-sided battle lasting less than two hours, the carrier was hit by salvo after salvo. In the end she turned over and sank, taking all the pilots but two – both of No 46 Squadron – with her. The survivors, Squadron Leader Cross and Flight Lieutenant Jameson, spent several hours on a Carley float before being rescued and taken to the Faeroe Islands. Both eventually reached high rank in the Royal Air Force.

CHAPTER THREE

The Fighting French

On this side of the Channel, the best-remembered French fighter aces of World War Two are those who fought with the Royal Air Force after the collapse of France; pilots such as Pierre Clostermann and René Mouchotte, whose exploits were widely publicised in the post-war years. But there were many others who rose to fame in the cauldron of the Battle of France, who fought with courage and distinction during those blazing six weeks between the onset of the German *Blitzkrieg* on 10 May 1940 and the armistice of 24 June, and yet who remain relatively – if not completely – unknown outside their own country.

One such was Sergent Le Nigen of Groupe de Chasse (Fighter Group) GC III/3, which was equipped with Morane 406 fighters. The Morane, which was roughly the equivalent of the RAF's Hawker Hurricane in terms of its design and development history, was cannon-armed and manoeuvrable, but it was under-powered, with a top speed of barely 300 mph, and unlike the Hurricane it was inferior to the Messerschmitt 109 on almost every count.

Le Nigen discovered this to his cost when, on 2 March 1940 – during the 'Phoney War' period that preceded the German onslaught – he and two other pilots were detailed to fly an escort mission for a Potez 63 reconnaissance aircraft over the Saar. Three more Moranes from another unit were flying top cover.

Over the front line the Moranes were bounced by an estimated 25 Me 109s and a vicious, one-sided dogfight developed, starting at 25,000 feet and quickly descending to lower altitudes. One of Le Nigen's colleagues, Sergent Ribo, was soon shot down in flames and Le Nigen himself was subjected to a succession of violent attacks that riddled his Morane with cannon shells and shot his undercarriage hydraulics to pieces. Using all his skill, he managed to escape and brought his crippled aircraft down for a belly-landing on the airfield at Nancy.

Le Nigen's brief war began in earnest on 19 May, when his was one of nine Morane's patrolling the Guise-Le Catteau area at dawn. The aircraft were flying at 15,000 feet and the mission was hampered by very poor radio communications, which made it virtually impossible for the pilots to report any enemy aircraft they sighted. Suddenly, Le Nigen's Morane went into a steep dive. The other pilots followed, realising that the tall, fair-haired Breton must have spotted something. A minute later they saw his aircraft flatten out a few feet above the forest below, and only then did they sight his target: a Henschel 126 observation aircraft. Le Nigen opened fire at point-blank range and climbed away steeply as the German aircraft fell blazing among the trees.

During a second mission that morning, nine more Moranes – again with Le Nigen – encountered 25 Dornier 17 bombers, escorted by twelve Me 109s, in the Cambrai-Le Quesnoy area. Le Nigen, ignoring two 109s that clung to his tail, shot down a third and escaped from the others by a series of tight turns, which the German fighters could not match. When he got back to base, he found that several bullets had pierced his cockpit without touching him; he had been lucky.

The next day, the pilots of GC III/3 were at readiness at Beauvais when fifteen Heinkel 111 bombers escorted by 25 twin-engined Me 110 fighters were reported to be approaching the airfield. By the time the Frenchmen reached their aircraft, the enemy formation was already in sight. Le Nigen was first off, just as the German bombs were starting to explode on the airfield. Meanwhile, the Me 110s were strafing anti-aircraft positions around the perimeter. Le Nigen, turning hard at very low level, fired at a 110 and saw it break up, its debris falling just outside the airfield, and then – joined now by the other French fighter pilots – pursued the remaining 110s, which were heading away

26

towards the east. After a few minutes Le Nigen and the others returned to Beauvais, swearing fluently; their Moranes had been unable to catch up with the 110s.

Le Nigen's score continued to mount during the remainder of May. Early in June the final remnants of the British Expeditionary Force were evacuated from Dunkirk; the French fought on south of the Somme, and now at last GC III/3 exchanged their tired Moranes for a new type of fighter, the Dewoitine 520. The D.520 was vastly superior to the Morane, but it was not available in sufficient numbers to influence the course of the air war over France. Only four fighter groups were equipped with it, but between them they destroyed 114 enemy aircraft, together with 39 probably destroyed. The cost was high; 85 D.520s were lost and 44 pilots killed.

Le Nigen's last mission was flown on 16 June, when the German armies were thrusting towards the Loire. At 12.55 hours, seven D.520s – all that remained serviceable with GC III/3 – took off from Grand Malleray to carry out an offensive patrol in the Auxerre area. As they arrived over the airfield at Auxerre, Le Nigen suddenly announced over the radio that he could see several German aircraft on it. The other pilots received the news with incredulity; they knew that Auxerre had been occupied by French forces only an hour earlier. But Le Nigen was right. There were four Henschel 126s on the base, one of which was seen to be taking off. Le Nigen broke away and shot it down. It was his twelfth and last victory. The other pilots also dived down to strafe the remaining Henschels, destroying all three.

That same day, GC III/3 was ordered to withdraw to Perpignan. A few days later, with the Franco-German armistice imminent, the pilots flew their D.520s across the Mediterranean to Fez, in Morocco. There, on 15 July 1940, Sergent Le Nigen was decorated with the Medaille Militaire in recognition of his exploits during the Battle of France.

Soon afterwards, Le Nigen was admitted to hospital suffering from acute stomach pains. A few days later, he died of peritonitis. Within hours of his death, it was announced that he had been granted a commission in the French Air Force.

Le Nigen was the fourth-ranking French ace of 1940, and the only one to gain most of his victories while flying the Morane

27

406. The three aces above him, and the five below, scored all their successes while flying a sturdy American-built fighter, the Curtiss Hawk 75A. An initial order for 100 of these machines had been placed in May 1938, and in 1939 – when it became obvious that the output of the French aircraft industry was incapable of matching German fighter production – follow-on orders were placed for a further 235 aircraft. During the Battle of France the Hawk equipped, or partially equipped, five fighter groups, which between them claimed 311 victories.

The largest Hawk unit at the beginning of the Battle of France was Escadre de Chasse 5, with 111 aircraft assigned. One of its fighter groups was GC I/5, which was commanded by a very talented pilot named Capitaine Jean Accart. Born in Fecamp, Accart began his career as a seaman officer in the French Merchant Navy, serving on steam packets of the Compagnie General Transatlantique before transferring to the French Navy in 1932. In 1936 Lieutenant de Vaisseau Accart changed his allegiance yet again, this time to the French Air Force, where he soon gained his flying brevet.

For Jean Accart, the fighting began on the very first day of the German onslaught, at dawn on 10 May 1940, when he took off on a patrol with a Czech pilot named Perina. His own words tell the story:

'Rising out the shadows in a rapid climb, with no instructions from fighter control, I set course eastwards, where I could see a cluster of condensation trails lit up by the rising sun. With Perina a little lower down and astern, I climbed flat out towards them but was unable to reach them, so I set up a patrol in the Second Army's sector, between Sedan and Verdun. The sun was well up when I spotted fifteen black dots, creeping westwards and to the south of our position. We headed for them, gaining altitude, for they were clearly higher than us. After a few minutes, we were close enough to identify them positively as Messerschmitt 110s.

'At that moment, they began a wide turn towards us. We were still a few hundred metres below them and I didn't think that they had seen us, because our aircraft camouflage would be blending in with the terrain below. They continued their gentle turn and I decided that they had not seen us, so I gave the order to attack. We were only two against fifteen, so there was time for only one quick pass, firing on the climb. I broke away as a group of five Messerschmitts turned towards me and looked for Perina, but he was nowhere to be seen. I found out later that he had continued to fire in the climb for too long and had dropped away in a spin.

'Those twin-engined Messerschmitts were pretty manoeuvrable, but I got away by gaining altitude. The enemy formation seemed to have broken up in confusion, all except for a group of five which had formed up in line astern. I attacked this group head-on and fired on the leading aircraft, which was also firing at me. I passed underneath him and fired on each of the others in turn. It was all over in just a few seconds. The last one in line pulled up just as I opened fire and I broke hard in case of a sudden attack from astern, but to my surprise the Messerschmitts regrouped and flew off to the east. I counted twelve and looked for the others; I couldn't see them against the glare of the sun, but I did see Perina climbing up to rejoin me.

'I was making up my mind whether or not to chase the Germans when I heard Adjutant [Warrant Officer] Bouvard call over the radio to say that he was engaging a group of Dorniers near Reims, flying at 3,000 metres. Bouvard, who was accompanied by Sous-Lieutenant [Pilot Officer] Goupy, shot down one of the bombers, but then Goupy got an incendiary bullet in the thigh and just managed to make a forced landing at Wez-Thuisy before losing consciousness. Perina and I dived flat out towards the Dorniers, which were soon in sight, and attacked the bomber on the far left of the formation. He began to smoke, lost altitude and splashed himself all over a field near Suippes. . .

'Events unfolded at an infernal pace throughout the day. We had hardly been refuelled when we were ordered off to escort some Potez 63s which were carrying out a reconnaissance over the Ardennes. We passed over the enemy columns which were pushing westwards and had to dodge some severe flak. . .Back at Suippes we were placed on alert. Two hours went by, and I was just about to hand over to someone else when a flare shot up from the command post, ordering us to take off. Just as I got airborne, with Perina following, the airfield was carpeted with bomb-bursts. Looking up, I saw what seemed to be a mixture of Dornier 17s and Messerschmitt 110s, dead overhead at about 3,000 metres.

'A furious battle developed. In the space of a few seconds I fired on a Dornier, went to the aid of a Curtiss that was being attacked by two Messerschmitts, and shot down a second Dornier just outside Suippes. Then, with Perina still clinging to me, I crept up behind a Dornier hidden under his tail, and fired a long burst into him, yawing a little so as to rake him from wingtip to wingtip. I was close enough to see the bullet strikes. I ceased firing and throttled back in order not to overshoot the target. The bomber's motors were still turning, but I saw one of the crew jump, his parachute opening as he swept past me. I pulled off to the right a little to watch the Dornier, and at the same time to keep an eye on some enemy fighters which were approaching.

'I saw a second crew member jump, but his parachute opened too soon and became snagged on the fuselage. I watched him struggling to free himself, trying to drag himself along the shroud lines towards the canopy. He pulled himself forward a little, then lost his grip and slid back towards the tail. The Dornier began to smoke, the pilot baled out and the bomber went into a vertical dive, dragging the trapped man with it. It impacted with a terrific explosion on the banks of a little river.

'I returned to Suippes with Perina as dusk was falling, after having destroyed another Dornier near Dun-sur-Meuse. So, for me, ended the first day of the battle. . .'

Accart went on to destroy a total of twelve enemy aircraft, with three probables, before the battle ended in June. He was severely wounded in the closing stages and spent a long time in hospital before crossing the Pyrenees into Spain in 1942, together with a number of trainee fighter pilots. He eventually reached North Africa, where he was given command of a fighter group. Following the allied victory in North Africa in 1943, this unit was transferred to the Royal Air Force and became No 345 Squadron, subsequently operating in Normandy and Belgium. Jean Accart reached high rank in the French Air Force after the war, commanding France's Tactical Air Forces in the early 1960s.

However, it was Accart's deputy in GC I/5, Lieutenant Edmond Marin la Meslée, who became France's top-scoring fighter ace in 1940, accumulating sixteen victories and four aircraft probably destroyed. Edmond Marin la Meslée established his reputation as a first-rate fighter pilot during the 'Phoney War', and one of his early air battles, in January 1940 is described in his own words:

'I was on patrol with my wingman, Sous-Lieutenant Rey, at 8,000 metres when I suddenly spotted a splendid Dornier 17, heading for Belgium about 200 metres below us and two kilometres away. I warned my wingman, then placed the sun at my back and attacked from astern. The German machine-gunner opened fire when I was about 400 metres away. . .I manoeuvred to throw him off his aim, closing all the time, and opened fire at 200 metres. I gave him several bursts, closing right in until I was obliged to break off and let my wingman have his turn. The German gunner was firing at me all the time, but his bullets went wide. I could see my own bullets hitting the Dornier's fuselage and engines, and some debris struck my aircraft.

'The Dornier flew straight on, and I came in for a second attack. More debris hit my aircraft, and oil spattered my windscreen. I thought that I had been hit and broke away, but just as Rey was preparing to fire the Dornier went into a vertical dive. He must have been hit pretty badly, because he was losing fuel and his engines were belching smoke. Rey fired inbz the dive, broke away, and I took over. The Dornier levelled out at 2,000 metres, then went into a dive once more and turned towards the frontier. We took it in turns to fire at him, not giving him a moment's respite. The German gunner was still firing and it seemed likely that the Dornier might escape, because we were very close to the border. I remember shouting words of encouragement to my wingman. We were now very close to the ground, so close in fact that I had to break off an attack. A moment later, I had the immense satisfaction of seeing the Dornier make a belly landing in a field. On returning to base I learned that he had come down only one kilometer from the frontier; the crew had been taken prisoner, and only one of them was wounded. My aircraft was unscathed, although my wingman's had been hit five times.'

After the Battle of France, Marin la Meslée escaped to North Africa with the other surviving pilots and eventually took command of GC I/5. In August 1944 this unit, equipped now with American P-47 Thunderbolts, took part in the invasion of southern France. On 4 February 1945, while carrying out a ground attack mission against enemy ground forces near Colmar, Edmond Marin la Meslée was shot down by flak and killed.

Another notable Curtiss Hawk pilot with GC I/5 was Sergent-Chef (Flight Sergeant) Morel, who destroyed ten enemy aircraft in a single week between 10 and 18 May 1940. During an attack on a Heinkel 111 formation on 18 May, he was hit at close range by return fire and received a bullet in the head. He remained conscious long enough to bale out, but died during the descent. It was thought at the time that he had been shot by a French infantryman in the mistaken belief that he was a German, but a subsequent examination of his wrecked aircraft revealed a bullet hole in the windscreen.

Another Curtiss Hawk unit was GC II/4. During the first few days of the battle many of its aircraft were destroyed on the ground, so that only seven Hawks out of a normal complement of 34 remained serviceable on the morning of 15 May. Nevertheless, the Group gave a good account of itself in action that day, as its diary tells:

'Wednesday, 15 May 1940. At dawn, while we were establishing ourselves in our new location, we were briefed to fly an air cover mission south-west of Charleroi. Take-off was fixed for 11.00. All available aircraft were to take part; there were only seven. The pilots were selected from the 3rd and 4th Escadrilles: Lieutenant Vincotte, Sous-Lieutenant Baptizet, Sous-Lieutenant Plubeau and Adjudant Tesseraud from the 4th, Capitaine Guieu, Adjudant Paulhan and Sergent-Chef Casenobe from the 3rd.

'We climbed without incident until we were over Reims, when we saw a superb V of nine twin-engined bombers heading south-west at 4,000 metres. We decided to attack. They were escorted by half a dozen Messerschmitt 109s, 1,000 metres higher up and a little behind. Lieutenant Vincotte attacked, perhaps a little too soon. The Messerschmitts came down on us and we were forced to break away and dive for safety. Only Lieutenant Vincotte stuck to the bombers and made several passes at the left-hand one (a Junkers 88). Meanwhile, Plubeau, Tesseraud and Baptizet were involved in a fierce dogfight with the 109s; each shot down an enemy fighter and then climbed rapidly to the aid of Vincotte. Together, they shot down one bomber; the remainder dropped their bombs haphazardly near Warmeriville and we went after them.

'Plubeau's cockpit was shattered by an explosive shell and he was forced to bale out. Vincotte damaged a second Junkers, then he too was hit in his fuel tanks and also had to bale out as his cockpit was filling with fumes and his oxygen equipment was out of action. Meanwhile, Baptizet, Guieu and Casenobe had spotted a Henschel 126 at low altitude, which they attacked and shot down in the forest of Silly l'Abbaye.

In the process Guieu flew through a treetop at full throttle; by some miracle he managed to reach base and land safely with great gashes torn in his wings.'

Regis Guieu was the only pilot of GC II/4 to become an ace in the Battle of France, scoring five victories. He was shot down and killed in a fight with Me 109s on 7 June, while escorting a Potez 63 reconnaissance aircraft near Soissons.

Another Curtiss Hawk ace with five victories was Lieutenant Houzé of GC II/5. He too lost his life during the Battle of France, but under very different circumstances. On 6 June, he was attacking an Me 110 when his own aircraft was hit and set on fire. Baling out, he landed in no-man's land and was picked up by French motor-cycle troops who were acting as rearguard. Refusing to be evacuated, Houzé seized a machine-pistol and took command of a group of French soldiers. By this time the rearguard was surrounded, and took refuge in a small wood. Houzé led his men in an attempted break-out, shooting dead several German soldiers who were lying in wait on the edge of the wood. The Frenchmen got clear, but Houzé was mortally wounded and died two hours later.

In all, ten of the sixteen French pilots who became aces during the Battle of France scored their victories while flying Curtiss Hawks. Four more flew with units operating the Bloch 152, a radial-engined fighter with a top speed of 316 mph and an armament of two cannon and two machine-guns. In action, the Bloch 152s scored 146 confirmed kills and 34 probables; the record was held by GC I/8, with 36 kills and four probables. Top-scoring Bloch 152 pilots were Sous-Lieutenant Thollon of GC I/8, with seven kills and one probable; Sergent Teillet of I/1 (seven plus one); Capitaine Couteaud of GC I/1 (six plus two); and Lieutenant Daval of GC II/9, with six. However, the Bloch 152 was inferior to the Me 109 on almost every count, and every Bloch-equipped unit engaged in the battle during May suffered heavy losses. 'Between 10 and 16 May,' wrote one 152 pilot, 'the rhythm of battle assumed a sinister monotone. We would take off with six, eight or nine aircraft and come back with two or three. Sometimes, some of the missing pilots would return to base after making a forced landing, often after having run out of fuel. The Bloch had an endurance of only one hour at normal cruise, and 45 minutes at full throttle.' The only French ace to score all his five victories while flying the Dewoitine D.520 was Sergent-Chef (later Capitaine) Le Gloan of GC III/6. All his kills were Italian aircraft, and he destroyed them in one air battle on 15 June, five days after Mussolini – sensing a quick victory and anticipating a share in the spoils – declared war on France and Great Britain.

The pilots of GC III/6 were just landing at Luc-en-Provence after a patrol over Marseille when a formation of Fiat BR.20 bombers, escorted by Fiat CR.42 biplane fighters, appeared overhead. Commandant Paul Stehlin, III/6's commander, at once ordered those pilots who had not yet landed to engage the enemy. The first pilot to do so was Le Gloan, who attacked a flight of CR.42s which was trying to gain altitude. Within seconds, two of the Italian fighters were spinning down in flames. Le Gloan's comrades stood on the airfield below and watched, spellbound, as he destroyed a third and fourth CR.42 in quick succession. He then went after a BR.20, which he also shot down. The crew of the latter aircraft, together with one of the CR.42 pilots, baled out and was dined by the officers of GC III/6 before going off into their brief captivity. For his exploit, Le Gloan received immediate promotion to Sous-Lieutenant.

After the fall of France, Pierre Le Gloan escaped to France with GC III/6. The unit, still with its D.520s, was later transferred to Rayak, in Syria, as part of the armed forces of the Vichy French regime there. In the summer of 1941, when a mixed force of British Empire and Free French troops invaded Syria and the Lebanon to secure these territories against Axis intervention, with its consequent dire threat to the vital Suez Canal, Le Gloan found himself in action again, this time against former allies. On 8 June 1941, the day the invasion began, Le Gloan shot down an RAF Hurricane over Damascus, and on the following day he destroyed two more. On the 15th he claimed a Gloster Gladiator, but in the air battle his D.520 was damaged and he crash-landed at Rayak.

On 23 June, Le Gloan was one of nine pilots of GC III/6 who took off to intercept RAF Hurricanes of No 80 Squadron which were strafing Rayak. He shot down two of them, but was himself hit and slightly wounded. He returned to action on 5 July and shot down another Hurricane. It was his seventh and last victory in the Syrian Campaign, during which he had shown himself to be the best fighter pilot on either side. Shortly afterwards, with Vichy resistance in Syria collapsing, Le Gloan was evacuated to Algeria with the surviving pilots of GC III/6.

Under the terms of the armistice, any French servicemen wishing to leave Syria for the parent country, or the French colonies in North Africa, were allowed to do so. Some, however, preferred to remain and fight for the Allied cause. On 1 September 1942, a unit known as Groupe de Chasse 3 was formed with British assistance at Rayak and given the title of the 'Régiment Normandie'. Two months later, the entire complement of 72 officers and men – their numbers increased by personnel trained in Britain – was transferred to Russia and equipped with Yakovlev Yak-1 fighters. The Regiment Normandie went into action on the Orel Front on 22 February 1943 under the leadership of Commandant Jean Tulasne, who was to score four kills before his death in action, and on 5 April Capitaine Albert Preziosi destroyed the unit's first enemy aircraft. Preziosi was also to gain four victories before he too was killed in action. The regiment was based less than fifteen miles from the front line, which enabled the pilots to fly a large number of tactical support missions. By September 1943 the regiment's score had risen to 40 enemy aircraft destroyed, and the French pilots subsequently took part in the bitter air fighting over Smolensk, Yelnya and Vitebsk. During the last months of 1943, they accounted for a further 77 German aircraft for the loss of 23 of their own number.

In the summer of 1944 the Régiment Normandie, which was now equipped with Yak-9 fighters, enjoyed spectacular successes, destroying a further 30 German aircraft between 22 June and the end of August. In September and October, the French pilots were engaged in a bitter period of air fighting over the Niemen and East Prussia; on one memorable day in October, led by Lieutenant-Colonel Pierre Pouyade (six victories) they destroyed no fewer than 26 enemy aircraft for no loss to themselves. The exploit earned them the honorary title of the Normandie-Nieman Regiment, and they were cited in a special Red Army Order of the Day – an honour reserved for outstanding achievements in battle.

In all, 38 of the Régiment Normandie's pilots became aces during the war on the Eastern Front. The top-scoring pilot was Capitaine Marcel Albert, with 23.

On their aircraft, the pilots of the Régiment Normandie carried the white Cross of Lorraine and a blue, white and red roundel. In their deeds, as the words of General Charles de Gaulle told the world, they carried the glory of France.

CHAPTER FOUR

The Battle of Britain Aces

On 2 September 1940, a Hurricane pilot was on patrol over Dover when he sighted two Messerschmitt 109s. He attacked one of them head-on. At a range of 100 yards the 109 broke away and the Hurricane pilot turned after it, firing several bursts into it. The 109 began to stream smoke and went down to crash two miles from Dover.

It was the pilot's first victory over England, but he already had eleven German aircraft to his credit in other skies. His name was Josef Frantisek, and he had been a Czech regular airman when the Germans occupied his country in the spring of 1939. He escaped to Poland, where he flew and fought with the Polish Air Force in September 1939, scoring his first victories against the *Luftwaffe*. After Poland's collapse he escaped to Romania, where he was interned, but he managed to escape and made his way through the Balkans to Syria, where he took ship for France.

During the battles of May and June 1940, flying Morane 406 fighters with the French Air Force, he added to his score and was awarded the *Croix de Guerre*. When France fell, Frantisek escaped again, this time to England, and after converting to Hurricanes he was posted to No 303 (Polish) Squadron at RAF Northolt. This unit, known as the *Kosciuszko* Squadron, was one of the first two Polish fighter units to reach operational readiness in Britain, and went into action at a crucial time of the Battle of Britain. (147

Polish pilots were to take part in the Battle, and 30 would lose their lives.)

Frantisek was the only Czech pilot on the squadron, but he did not seem to mind; he was very much a lone wolf by nature, and many of his successes were gained while flying lone patrols. He gained his second victory, an Me 109, on 3 September, and two days later, in a hectic engagement with 50 Me 109s and Ju 88s over the Thames Estuary, he added two more enemy aircraft to his tally. Disposing of an Me 109 which attacked him and overshot, he joined his flight commander, Flight Lieutenant Forbes, in an assault on the bomber formation, and sent a Ju 88 down into the sea. The next day, he destroyed an Me 109 over Sevenoaks.

His score continued to mount steadily during the remainder of September. On the last day of the month, he shot down an Me 109, his seventeenth victory over England. A few days later, on 8 October, he was landing after an early morning patrol when his Hurricane's wingtip struck a slight rise in the ground and somersaulted on its back. The fighter exploded in flames and its pilot, trapped in the cockpit, had no chance of escape. No other Czech fighter pilot was to surpass his score of 28 victories, and he was to remain the top-scorer of the Battle of Britain.

Close behind Frantisek, with sixteen confirmed victories, was Flying Officer Eric Lock of No 41 Squadron, which was based at RAF Catterick in North Yorkshire at the start of the Battle of Britain. His first combat came on 15 August 1940, when the *Luftwaffe* sent its bombers over from Norway and Denmark to attack RAF airfields in the north. Lock's combat report describes what happened:

'I was flying in formation with 41 Squadron when we were ordered to patrol north of base at 20,000 feet. After flying for a while we saw a formation of Junkers 88 and Messerschmitt 110. The squadron then went into line astern and we made an attack. During our second attack, I fired two short bursts into the starboard engine of a Messerschmitt 110. I followed it down to 10,000 feet, firing at the fuselage. The machine-gunner stopped firing. Continuing my dive I fired at the port engine, which caught fire. I left it at 5,000 feet still in a vertical dive, with both engines on fire.'

Lock did not see his victim crash, but a fellow pilot saw it plunge into Seaham Harbour.'

Lock got into the thick of the fighting in the first week of September, when No 41 Squadron moved to RAF Hornchurch in Essex. On 5 September, he destroyed two Heinkel 111s and a Messerschmitt 109, and the next day he shot down a Ju 88 into the Channel. Three days later he destroyed two Me 109s over Kent, and on 11 September he shot down a Ju 88 and an Me 110. This brought his total kills so far to nine, all of them confirmed; he had destroyed eight of the enemy aircraft in one week, a feat that brought him the award of a DFC. He went on to destroy seven more aircraft before the Battle officially ended, and shared in the destruction of another, bringing his tally to sixteen.

On 17 November, by which time he had scored six more kills, Lock was badly wounded in a battle over the Thames Estuary. He brought his Spitfire down to a crash-landing at Martlesham Heath and was hospitalised until May 1941, during which time he was awarded the DSO. In June 1941, having undergone fifteen operations for the removal of shell splinters from his right arm and both legs, he was pronounced fit again and posted as a flight commander to No 611 Squadron, flying Spitfires from Hornchurch. Fighter Command was just beginning its 'sweeps' over occupied France, and during the next few weeks Lock added four more enemy aircraft to his score. He now had 26 victories. On 3 August 1941, he failed to return from an operation over northern France and was posted missing, presumed killed. No-one ever found out what had happened to him.

Three pilots vied for third place in the Battle of Britain, each shooting down fifteen aircraft. They were Sergeant J.H. 'Ginger' Lacey of No 501 Squadron, Flying Officer Brian Carberry of No 603, and Pilot Officer Bob Doe of No 234. Lacey was already a very experienced fighter pilot when the Battle began, having destroyed five enemy aircraft in the Battle of France, and he briefly made the headlines of 13 September 1940, when he shot down a Heinkel 111 that had just bombed Buckingham Palace, but apart from that his achievements were mostly overlooked. For the popular Press, there was little mileage in the activities of a mere sergeant pilot. For the same reason, the exploits of Josef Frantisek remained relatively unknown until long afterwards. Ginger Lacey ended the war as a squadron leader, with 28 German and Japanese aircraft to his credit; but more important, perhaps, than his personal achievement in this respect was his skill as an air combat instructor. Few of the fighter pilots who were put through the mill by Ginger Lacey were ever taken by surprise by the enemy, and several went on to achieve respectable scores in their own right. They thought the world of him.

A score of 28 victories placed Ginger Lacey in joint eighth place in the pecking order of RAF fighter aces. Another who shared the position with him was Frank Carey, a contemporary of Lacey's who also fought in the Battles of France and Britain but who, unlike Lacey, rose from sergeant pilot to squadron leader in the space of six months. Carey first saw action with No 43 Squadron at RAF Acklington, Northumberland, early in 1940, when he shared in the destruction of a Heinkel 111; a few days later he shot another Heinkel down in flames over the North Sea. At the end of February he was awarded the DFM, commissioned, and posted to No 3 Squadron, which rotated flights of Hurricanes to France when the *Blitzkrieg* began.

During the Battle of France Carey destroyed four enemy aircraft, together with two probables, before being wounded on 14 May. On his return to England he was posted back to No 43 Squadron as a flight commander, and destroyed an Me 109 over the Channel on 19 June. During July Carey added two more aircraft – an Me 109 and an Me 110 – to his score. Then, in August, the Battle of Britain began in earnest. On 12 and 13 August, the first two days of heavy *Luftwaffe* attacks on the RAF airfields in the south of England, Carey claimed two Junkers 88s, and on the 16th he was involved in a fierce air battle over the south coast. His combat report describes the action:

'I was leading "A" Flight behind the leader of the squadron, having taken off at 12.45 hours to patrol Selsey Bill at 11,000 feet when I gave Tally Ho on sighting waves of Ju 87s. The leader ordered the squadron to attack one formation of 87s from the front and immediately on closing the leader of the enemy aircraft was hit by Squadron Leader and crew baled out.

'I pulled my flight over to the left to attack the right hand formation as we met them. Almost as soon as I opened fire, the enemy aircraft's crew baled out and the machine crashed in the sea, just off Selsey Bill. I turned to continue my attack from the rear as enemy aircraft were completely broken up by frontal attack and several other waves behind me turned back out to sea immediately although we had not attacked

40

them. I picked out one Ju 87 and fired two 2-second bursts at him and the enemy aircraft burst into flames on the port wing root. I did not wait to see it crash as I turned to attack another. After one burst at the third enemy aircraft, two large pieces of metal broke off the port wing and the enemy aircraft seemed to stop abruptly and go into a dive, but I did not see the machine crash as two other Ju 87s were turning on to my tail. I eventually picked on a fourth, but after firing two bursts and causing the engine to issue black smoke, the enemy aircraft turned out to sea and I ran out of ammunition. I noticed firing behind me and turned to see a pair of Me 109s behind me, one firing and the other apparently guarding his tail. After a few evasive actions enemy aircraft broke off and I returned to land and refuel and rearm at 13.40 hours.'

Two days later, while leading No 43 Squadron on patrol, Carey encountered another large formation of Ju 87s near Chichester. He shot down one Stuka, but his own aircraft was repeatedly hit by machine-gun fire and he was wounded in the right knee. He brought his Hurricane down for a successful forced landing, and spent the next couple of weeks recuperating.

Frank Carey ended the Battle of Britain with a total score of 18 enemy aircraft destroyed. In 1941 he was appointed to command the newly-formed No 135 Squadron, and on 6 December that year this unit sailed for Rangoon – just in time to meet the Japanese offensive in Burma. It was there he scored his last ten victories, his operational flying in World War Two ending in May 1943.

The end of the war found Carey at the Central Fighter Establishment as Group Captain (Tactics). With hostilities over, he reverted to the rank of wing commander, and in 1948–9 he was Wing Commander (Flying) at RAF Gutersloh in Germany, where No 135 Wing operated Hawker Tempest IIs and, later, de Havilland Vampires. Promoted once more to group captain, he held a number of other appointments within RAF Fighter Command before joining the UK Joint Services Liaison Staff as Air Adviser to the High Commissioner in Australia, a post he held from 1958 to 1960. On his retirement from the RAF he decided to stay in Australia and became a senior representative for Rolls-Royce Ltd in Canberra.

Although Frank Carey officially ended his war with a score of 28 enemy aircraft destroyed, many of his colleagues believed that the actual figure was much higher. The problem was that although he scored several kills during the long retreat through Burma in 1942, these could not be confirmed officially as No 135 Squadron's records were lost or destroyed. Some sources claim that his total score could be as high as fifty. If that is so, it would make Frank Carey the top-scoring British Commonwealth or American fighter pilot to emerge from the Second World War. The exact figure, however, will never be known.

One of the top-scoring pilots during the Battle of Britain was a Pole, Squadron Leader Witold Urbanowicz, who destroyed fourteen enemy aircraft. Like so many of his fellow countrymen, Urbanowicz had reached Britain via the Balkans and France, and after operational training he was posted to No 303 Kosciuszko Squadron. He gained his first victory on 15 August, when, on patrol over the Channel off Portsmouth, he caught an Me 109, pursued it out to sea and shot it down. Soon afterwards he was given command of No 303 Squadron's 'A' Flight, and then, when the squadron commander was killed, he was promoted to lead the unit. Under his command, the pilots of No 303 Squadron soon distinguished themselves. On 31 August, six Hurricanes of 'A' Flight engaged some Me 109s escorting bombers, and destroyed four of them for no loss to themselves, and on 7 September, intercepting a formation of Dornier 17s attacking London docks, the Poles were credited with sixteen per cent of the enemy aircraft destroyed by Fighter Command that day. Three of the Polish squadron's own aircraft were lost in the battle, and two pilots wounded.

On 11 September, No 303 Squadron claimed fourteen victories for the loss of two of its own pilots. On 26 September, during a visit by King George VI, the squadron was scrambled to intercept enemy bombers attacking Portsmouth and the pilots claimed the destruction of eleven enemy aircraft – a great success, particularly as the King was following proceedings in the operations room. During the critical month of September No 303 Squadron was credited with just over eleven per cent of all enemy aircraft destroyed by the RAF – the highest score for any unit in Fighter Command, and more than double that achieved by the nearest rival.

Witold Urbanowicz's last combat in the Battle of Britain took place on 30 September, and it was his best day yet. Leading his squadron into action over Kent, he destroyed a Dornier 17 and then came up behind two Me 109s, which failed to see him until it was too late. Closing right in, he gave each of them a short burst and sent them down into the Channel.

For his exploits in the Battle, Urbanowicz was awarded the DFC, the *Virtuti Militari,* Poland's highest decoration, and the Cross of Valour, the Polish equivalent of the DFC. In 1941, he was appointed CO of the Polish Fighter Wing in the RAF, but flew only a few more missions until he was sent to Washington as Assistant Air Attaché. In 1943, he transferred to the USAAF and flew on operations with the 14th Air Force. He left the USAAF in 1946 and took out US citizenship.

Another pilot who scored 14 kills during the Battle of Britain was a New Zealander, Flying Officer (later Flight Lieutenant) Colin Gray, who flew Spitfires in No 54 Squadron alongside another New Zealander, Flying Officer Alan Deere. Whereas Deere, who was later to lead the famous Biggin Hill Wing on fighter sweeps and escort missions over France in 1943, was much publicised, Gray's achievements went largely unrecorded until long after the war.

Colin Gray's first taste of action came over Dunkirk in May 1940, when he shared in the destruction of an Me 109. His next victory came on 24 July, during the preliminary phase of the Battle of Britain, when he shot down an Me 109 over Margate. When the main battle began on 12 August, Gray destroyed two Me 109s, and repeated this success three days later. On 18 August he attacked an Me 110 and sent it down on fire, and later that day he crippled an Me 109 which crashed in the middle of Clacton. On 24 August he chased an Me 110 almost all the way across the Channel and shot it down off the French coast, and two days later he added an Me 109 to his score. In the four days from 31 August to 3 September he destroyed six more enemy aircraft and had a number of lucky escapes, one when a cannon shell exploded behind his cockpit without injuring him. On his last day of action No 54 Squadron was sent north to RAF Catterick for a rest, which probably saved his life.

Colin Gray, who later reached the rank of group captain, subsequently fought over France, in Malta and North Africa. His official final score was 27½ enemy aircraft destroyed.

While the Air Ministry remained reluctant to publicise the exploits of the leading fighter pilots in the Battle of Britain, the Germans had no such scruples. Two names, those of Werner Mölders and Adolf Galland – whose respective number of victories reached 54 and 52 by the end of the Battle of Britain – were featured constantly in the German propaganda organs. But it was a young fighter pilot who had been one of Mölders' pupils in the 1930s who surpassed both of them.

A forester's son, Helmut Wick had been a poor scholar as a child, constantly playing truant to escape into the woods. His sole ambition, then, had been to follow in his father's footstep, but in 1936 he joined the new *Luftwaffe* and, under the instruction of Mölders and other skilled pilots, he soon showed exceptional flying talent. He scored his first kill in November 1939, during the 'Phoney War' period, and when the Battle of France began his score mounted with phenomenal speed. He was aggressive and impetuous, and intensely patriotic. His unit was JG 2 'Richthofen', named after the celebrated flying ace of the previous war, and it was the ambition of every German fighter pilot to better Richthofen's score of 80 enemy aircraft destroyed.

At the end of October 1940, Helmut Wick's score stood at 49, and he was itching to catch up with his old instructor, Mölders. Wick, at the age of 25, was now commanding JG 2. On 6 November he led his Me 109s in a fighter sweep over the Southampton area of southern England, and a day or two later wrote this account of what happened.

'We met a formation of Hurricanes flying lower than ourselves. Just as I was about to start the attack, I saw something above me and immediately called on the intercom: "Look out, Spitfires ahead." The Spitfires were still far enough away to permit an attack on the lower-flying Hurricanes.

'At that moment the Hurricanes made a turn, which proved to be their downfall. We shot down four of this group, one of which fell to me. The remaining Hurricanes turned away but began to climb again, and during the climb I caught one of them flying on the right-hand side of the formation. The Hurricanes then dived steeply. I cannot fully explain my next experience – perhaps I was not quite fit or my nerves were frayed – but after my second Englishman went down, I only wanted to fly home.

I still had fuel for a few more minutes of action. . .I saw three Spitfires coming in from the sea in front of me. I saw them first and caught up with them quickly and the first one went down immediately. Now, I said to myself, we must get them all. If we let them get away they will probably kill some of my comrades tomorrow, now away with them!

'I gritted my teeth and started the next attack. The second Spitfire fell after a few bursts, leaving only one. . .I fired at him with my machine-guns and soon white smoke poured from him. The pilot appeared to be hit because the aircraft went down out of control, but suddenly it recovered and I was forced to attack it again. The Spitfire slowly turned over and crashed to the ground. Now it really was time to fly home. When I arrived back over my airfield, I did not perform the usual stunts to indicate my victories as my fuel was almost exhausted. When I jumped out of the aircraft I hugged the first person who came across to me, who by chance turned out to be an old friend from my training days. I have now scored 53 victories and need only one more to draw level with my old instructor Werner Mölders.'

The next day, Wick led 50 Me 109s on an offensive sweep over the Isle of Wight. They encountered the eleven Hurricanes of No 145 Squadron, which had just returned south to RAF Tangmere after a spell at Dyce, near Aberdeen. The 109s split up and boxed in the Hurricanes, whose pilots tried to escape by climbing. It was the signal for the 109s to dart in, attacking in pairs and picking off one Hurricane after another. Five Hurricanes were shot down, two of their pilots being killed, and Helmut Wick gained his 54th victory. On 28 November, he failed to return from a scrap between JG 2's Messerschmitts and RAF Spitfires over the Channel; it was later established that he had escaped from his crippled aircraft, but drowned.

Wick was succeeded as commander of JG 2 by Wilhelm Balthasar, another very experienced fighter pilot and splendid leader, although his manner was less flamboyant than Wick's. Balthasar had fought in the Spanish Civil War, claiming six victories – four of which, Russian SB-2 bombers, he destroyed in six minutes on 7 February 1938 – and in the Battle of France he had shot down 21 aircraft in as many days. During the Battle of Britain he commanded III/JG 3, and recorded a combat that took place on 23 September 1940:

'Over London my *Schwarm* [flight] encountered a formation of about 60 Spitfires. I made a head-on attack on one of them. The enemy's tracer flew past my canopy, but the Englishman went spinning down in flames. Perhaps he had lost his nerve. Now a wild dogfight began. It was best to break away. Now I had four Spitfires on my tail. I was at 8,000 metres, and I pushed the stick forward and dived away at full speed, pulling out at ground level with my wings fluttering. No British fighter could have followed my wild dive. I looked behind me. Damn! There were two Spits on my tail again. There was no time to draw breath. My only chance of escape lay in my flying ability at low level, hedge-hopping to the Channel over houses and around trees. It was no use, one of them was always there and I couldn't shake him off. He hung a hundred metres behind me. Then we were over Dover. I thought; he can't keep this up, as I fled out over the wavetops, but the Spitfire stayed right behind.

'I jinked to right and left as the pilot opened fire and the bullets splashed into the water in front of me. I blinked the sweat out of my eyes. The French coast was now in sight. My fuel was getting low. I kept squinting behind so as not to miss the moment when he broke away. Wait, my friend, I thought, you must return soon, and then I will be the hunter.

'Cap Gris Nez loomed up in front, and I skimmed over it one metre above. Suddenly the Tommy climbed steeply and slowed down. At once I turned my Me 109 and zoomed up in a tight bank, engine howling, straight at him. I fired one burst from close range – I nearly rammed him – and the Spitfire went straight into the sea. He flew fantastically.'

Another Spanish Civil War veteran who fought in the Battle of Britain was Walter Oesau, who in July 1940 was *Staffelkapitän* (squadron leader) of 7/JG 51. One of his early successes was a Hurricane of No 111 Squadron, which he shot down on 10 July while escorting a force of Dorniers attacking British convoys; unfortunately, his jubilation was marred by the fact that the Hurricane collided with a Dornier on the way down, both aircraft crashing in the Channel. By 20 August, Oesau had scored 20 victories and been promoted to *Hauptmann* (captain). He took command of III/JG 51 towards the end of 1940, and later relieved Balthasar as *Kommandeur* of JG 2. Oesau, who already had eight victories in Spain, went on to achieve a total score of

125 enemy aircraft destroyed, 44 of them on the eastern front. He was killed in action on 11 May, 1944.

Herbert Ihlefeld also fought in Spain, destroying nine Republican aircraft. In August 1940, at the age of 27, he was commanding No 1 Squadron of the 2nd *Lehrgeschwader* (I/LG 2) which was based on the Channel coast and operating Me 109s; the *Lehrgeschwader*'s function was to test new equipment and tactics under combat conditions. On 13 September he was awarded the Knight's Cross for having gained 21 victories. Later, during the Russian campaign, he became the fifth German fighter pilot to claim more than 100 kills; he was to end the war with a total of 130 to his credit, including the nine in Spain. He died in January 1952.

On 14 September 1940, the day after Ihlefeld received his medal, Captain Joachim Müncheberg was also awarded the Knight's Cross. In 1939, as a lieutenant in III/JG 26, Müncheberg had opened his scoring by destroying a Bristol Blenheim reconnaissance aircraft over northern Germany. August 1940 found him commanding 7/JG 26, and a month later he had 20 victories. He was later transferred to the Mediterranean, where he claimed 19 RAF fighters destroyed during the attacks on Malta. In March 1943, by which time his total number of kills stood at 103, he was killed when his Me 109 collided with a Spitfire over Tunisia.

These were the men whom Hermann Göring, C-in-C *Luftwaffe,* called his 'Young Turks'; men who had been brought in to replace the veteran *Geschwader* commander early in the Battle of Britain. Some, like Adolf Galland, survived the war; most did not, although a few came very close to seeing the conflict through. One such was Günther 'Franzl' Lützow, who fought with JG 3 during the Battle of Britain. In January 1945 he had amassed 103 kills, 85 of them on the Russian Front. At that time, he was one of several senior *Luftwaffe* officers who were pressing both Hitler and Göring to use the Messerschmitt 262 jet in the interceptor role, rather than as a reprisal bomber; Göring flew into a rage, accused Lützow of mutiny and banished him to Italy, forbidding him to set foot on German soil again.

But Lützow did return, in the last weeks of the war; and it was in an Me 262, on 24 April 1945, that he met his end.

CHAPTER FIVE

Cover of Darkness

In air fighting by day, the secret of success was usually to see the enemy before he saw you, manoeuvre into a favourable attacking position, and then employ the correct set of tactics, depending on the circumstances. Night-fighting, however, was an entirely different matter. In the last two years of the war it was to develop into a very exact science, but in the early years, before technology gave the night-fighters the equipment they needed to seek and destroy their adversaries with growing accuracy, success depended to a great extent on being in the right place at the right time.

Before the outbreak of hostilities, very few of the belligerent air forces had given much thought to the development of an effective night-fighter force. In June 1940, when the Battle of France ended, the RAF had five squadrons assigned to night-fighting; these were equipped with Bristol Blenheims and two of them, Nos 29 and 604, were just starting to carry out trials with rudimentary AI (Airborne Interception) radar. During the Battle of France itself, the French Air Force had five night-fighter flights equipped with Potez 631s, but in six weeks of fighting they never carried out a night interception, all their engagements being fought during the day.

The *Luftwaffe*'s first night-fighter unit, IV/JG 2, was formed at Jever in February 1940, by which time – despite *Luftwaffe* C-in-C Hermann Göring's earlier boast that no enemy aircraft would ever fly over the territory of the Reich – RAF Bomber Command had already visited Germany on a number of occasions, either to attack shipping in the northern ports or to drop leaflets over the Ruhr. This unit was equipped with Messerschmitt 109s, day-fighters which were totally unsuited to night-fighting, and many were lost in accidents; all IV/JG 2 had to show on the credit side was a single British bomber, a Whitley engaged in leaflet-dropping, which was shot down in full moonlight conditions in March 1940. But in May 1940, two more *Luftwaffe* night-fighter groups were formed with twin-engined Messerschmitt 110s, and the nucleus of a dedicated night-fighter defence was established under Colonel Josef Kammhuber.

In Britain, AI radar developments proceeded well in the summer of 1940, and on the night of 23/24 July a radar-equipped Blenheim carrying out operational trials with the Fighter Interception Unit at RAF Tangmere intercepted and destroyed a Dornier 17 bomber. This was the first recorded success of a radar-assisted fighter, and although to some extent it was a lucky interception it showed that the concept was feasible, and the conversion of Blenheims to the night-fighter role continued.

However, many of the early night successes over Britain during the winter of 1940–41 were scored by pilots flying Spitfires or Hurricanes. Operating on a hit-or-miss basis, they would seek out enemy bombers trapped in the glare of searchlights and would then go into the attack, risking being shot down by friendly anti-aircraft fire.

One such pilot was Flight Lieutenant Richard Stevens, a Hurricane pilot with No 151 Squadron at RAF Manston. A former civil pilot who had flown the cross-Channel mail route at night and in all weathers, Stevens was 30 years old and a very experienced man by the time he joined No 151 Squadron at the tail-end of the Battle of Britain, in October 1940. At this time the Germans had switched most of their effort to night attacks, and night after night Stevens watched in frustration as the German bombers droned overhead towards the red glare of burning London. At last, one night in December, he sought permission to try his hand at intercepting the raiders, and it was granted.

His early night patrols were disappointing. For several nights running, although the Manston controller assured him that the sky was stiff with enemy bombers, Stevens saw nothing. Then, on the night of 15 January 1941, the shellbursts of the London anti-aircraft defences led him to a Dornier 17, which he chased up to 30,000 feet and then almost down to ground level in a screaming dive as the German pilot tried to shake him off. But Stevens hung on, and after two or three short bursts the bomber went down and exploded on the ground.

It was No 151 Squadron's first night victory, and there was more to come. On a second patrol that night, Stevens caught a Heinkel 111 at 17,000 feet, heading for London, and shot it down into the Thames Estuary. The night's work earned him a Distinguished Flying Cross.

Somehow, it seemed as though Stevens' brace of kills had been a good omen. After that, the RAF's night-fighter squadrons seemed to enjoy more success. Men like Flight Lieutenant John Cunningham of No 604 Squadron, now flying fast, heavily-armed Bristol Beaufighters, began to carve out reputations for themselves as bomber destroyers. Cunningham, known by the nickname of 'Cat's Eyes' bestowed on him by the popular press, and which he thoroughly detested, was to destroy no fewer than eight enemy bombers at night in April 1941, having been led expertly to his targets by his AI operator, Sergeant Jimmy Rawnsley. He was to end the war with a score of twenty enemy aircraft destroyed, two probably destroyed and seven damaged, most of them at night. (The 'Cat's Eyes' nickname, of course, was designed to divert attention from the Beaufighter's AI radar, which was still highly secret and about which the public as yet knew nothing.)

It was eyesight alone, however, with a little help from searchlights and shellbursts, that brought Richard Stevens to his victims. Shortly after the award of his DFC, he developed ear trouble and was grounded for a while, but he celebrated his return to action on 8 April 1941 by shooting down two Heinkel 111s in one night. Two nights later he got another Heinkel and a Junkers 88, and a few days later he received a Bar to his DFC. He destroyed yet another Heinkel on the 19th, and on 7 May he accounted for two more. Three nights after that, his claim was one Heinkel destroyed and one probably destroyed. He shot down a further Heinkel on 13 June, damaged one on the 22nd, and on 3 July sent a Junkers 88 down in flames. There seemed to be no end to his success; at this time he was the RAF's top-scoring night-fighter pilot, enjoying a considerable lead over pilots who flew the radar-equipped Beaufighters.

Stevens experienced a lot of frustration during the summer months of 1941. In June the Germans invaded Russia, and by the end of July they had withdrawn many of their bomber units from the Western Front. Raids at night over Britain became fewer, and although Stevens continued to fly his lone patrols, for weeks he never saw an enemy bomber. Then, one evening in October, he spotted a Junkers 88 slipping inland over the East Anglian coast and attacked it. The Junkers jettisoned its bombs and turned away, diving low over the water, but Stevens caught it with a burst of fire and sent it into the sea. It was his fourteenth victory.

Soon afterwards, Stevens was posted to another Hurricane unit, No 253 Squadron, as a flight commander, and he immediately set about devising a plan to take the war to the enemy by flying night intruder operations over the German airfields in Holland and Belgium. Later in the war, offensive operations of this kind would become routine, but in December 1941 Stevens was virtually pioneering a new technique. He flew his first night intruder operation on the night of 12/13 December, the day when it was announced that he had been awarded the Distinguished Service Order. He loitered in the vicinity of the bomber airfield at Gilze-Rijen, Holland, but saw no aircraft and returned home in disappointment.

Three nights later, he took off again, heading for the same destination, and never returned. The signal that his squadron commander sent to Group HQ was simple and concise. 'One Hurricane IIC (long range), 253 Squadron, took off Manston 19.40 hours, 15.12.41, to go to Gilze. It has failed to return and is beyond maximum endurance.' Somewhere out over darkened Europe, or more probably over the waters of the Channel, Richard Stevens, who had fought a lonely, single-handed battle in the night sky for a year, had met a lonely fate.

The majority of the home-based Hurricane II squadrons took part in night intruder operations at one time or another during 1942, and some became specialists in the role. No 1 Squadron, for example, which was based at RAF Tangmere, destroyed 22 enemy aircraft over occupied Europe between 1 April and

1 July that year before moving to Northumberland to convert to Typhoon fighter-bombers, and no fewer than fifteen of these victories were gained by one pilot, Flight Lieutenant Karel Kuttelwascher.

A highly competent and experienced pilot, Kuttelwascher – or 'Kut', as he was popularly known – had flown with the Czech Air Force for four years before his country was overrun by the Germans, after which he had made his way to Britain via France. He scored his first three kills – all Messerschmitt 109s – while flying convoy protection and bomber escort missions over the Channel in the spring and early summer of 1941, but it was when No 1 Squadron went over to night intruder operations in April 1942 that Kut really got into his stride. In April 1942 he destroyed three Junkers 88s, three Dornier 217s and a Heinkel 111, and on the night of 4/5 May he shot down three Heinkel 111s over St André. He destroyed a Dornier 217 off Dunkirk on 2/3 June, and on the following night he visited St André again to destroy a Heinkel 111 and a Dornier 217, as well as damaging another Dornier.

St André was once again the target on 21/22 June, when Kut shot down a Junkers 88 and damaged another. A Dornier 217 went before his guns near Trévières on 28/29 June, and his last two victims, also Dornier 217s, were brought down near Dinard on the night of 1/2 July, when he also damaged a third Dornier. That brought Kut's score to eighteen destroyed, with one probable (a Messerschmitt 109, his first combat in the RAF, on 2 February 1941) and five damaged. In addition, he may have claimed up to six victories while flying Morane 406 fighters in the Battle of France. After the war, he became a captain with British European Airways, flying Vikings and Elizabethans. He died of a heart attack on 17 August 1959, at the untimely age of 42.

No 1 Squadron's other leading scorer in the summer of 1942 was the squadron commander, Squadron Leader James MacLachlan, but with five enemy bombers destroyed and three damaged, MacLachlan was a long way behind his Czech colleague. A remarkable character, 'Mac' had scored six victories in the Battle of Britain and two more over Malta, but had himself been shot down in February 1941 and badly wounded, losing his left arm above the elbow. He took command of No 1 Squadron in November 1941, having been fitted with an artificial arm in the meantime. In June 1943, while flying a Mustang on a cross-Channel sweep, he and another Mustang pilot destroyed four Henschel 126 observation aircraft and two Junkers 88s in the space of ten minutes, Mac himself claiming three and a half. This brought his total score to 16½.

On 18 July 1943, again flying a Mustang across the Channel, Mac's aircraft was hit – possibly by small-arms fire – and crashed into a wood as he was trying to make a forced landing. He was still alive when the Germans found him, but died in hospital from severe head injuries a fortnight later.

Meanwhile, since the advent of the Bristol Beaufighter, night-fighter developments in the RAF had been making steady progress. Delays in the production of AI Mk IV radar equipment had prevented the full complement of five Beaufighter squadrons from becoming operational until the spring of 1941, but despite early teething troubles those that were operational had enjoyed some success. The first AI-assisted Beaufighter kill had in fact been claimed on the night of 19/20 November 1940, when Flight Lieutenant Cunningham and Sergeant Phillipson of No 604 Squadron were credited with the destruction of a Junkers 88, and by the time all five Beaufighter squadrons reached operational status their efficiency was greatly enhanced by the commissioning of six GCI (Ground Controlled Interception) radar stations on the south and east coasts of England. These could provide fairly wide coverage, and controllers could bring the fighter to within three miles of the target aircraft, at which point the AI Mk IV radar took over. The first GCI-controlled interception was made by John Cunningham on 12 January 1941, but was unsuccessful because the Beaufighter's guns jammed. Then, on 10 May 1941 – the last major *Luftwaffe* attack on London – GCI-controlled Beaufighters destroyed fourteen German bombers, the highest loss suffered by the *Luftwaffe* on any one night since the *Blitz* began.

Thirteen more Beaufighter squadrons were assigned to the night defence of Great Britain in 1941–2, and many of the RAF's night-fighter aces scored their early kills while flying the heavy twin-engined fighter. During the closing months of 1941 the *Luftwaffe*'s preoccupation with the eastern front meant that night raids on Britain were sporadic, but in the spring of 1942 the air offensive was renewed with the onset of the so-called 'Baedecker Raids', directed against Britain's historic cities.

By this time, the Beaufighter was beginning to be replaced as the RAF's primary night-fighting instrument by the de Havilland Mosquito, an aircraft whose long range and heavy armament of four 20-mm cannon made it highly suitable for the night intruder role, as well as for local night air defence. The intruder Mosquitos (and Beaufighters) were fitted with a device named 'Serrate' which, developed by the Telecommunications Research Establishment as a result of information on enemy night-fighting radars brought back by special countermeasures aircraft, enabled the British fighters to home in to the enemy's airborne radar transmissions. It had a range of about fifty miles, and was first used operationally in 1943 by No 141 Squadron, which scored 23 kills in three months with its help.

No 141 Squadron's commander was Wing Commander J.R.D. 'Bob' Braham, whose combat report describes a night action off the Dutch island of Ameland on the night of 17/18 August 1943. Braham was flying a Beaufighter Mk VI, and his navigator was Flight Lieutenant H. Jacobs.

'We took off from Coltishall at 22.00 hours on intruder patrol to Stade. We flew to a point north of Schiermonnikoog and then turned NE at 22.54. We continued on course for about five minutes when we sighted one Me 110 flying east and jinking. We turned and followed him towards the coast, closing in on the aircraft until we were at 300 yards range, 20 degrees starboard astern and a little below. Fire was opened with a two-second burst from all guns and strikes were seen all over the enemy aircraft. Smoke came from the port engine and the Me 110 dived to port. We gave him another two-second burst from 250 yards and he caught fire and dived into the sea, burning on the water. Immediately afterwards we saw a second Me 110 (which had been chasing us) a little above and turning gently to starboard on an easterly course. We gave a one-second burst of cannon and machine-gun at 50 yards in a gentle turn. The enemy aircraft appeared to blow up and we had to pull up and turn to port to avoid ramming it. At that point we saw one man bale out and his parachute open, and the enemy aircraft dived vertically into the sea in flames. . .we landed at Wittering at 01.45.'

Bob Braham, a pre-war regular RAF officer, had been involved in the development of night-fighting techniques since the beginning of the war, and he destroyed his first victim – a Dornier 17 – while flying a Blenheim of No 29 Squadron on 24 August 1940. By July 1941 he had four kills to his credit, all at night, and he increased this score to six by the end of the year. During this period, his radar operator was Sergeant Gregory, who was later commissioned. After a rest from operations (during which, incidentally, they destroyed a Dornier 217 in a Beaufighter 'borrowed' while on a visit to their old squadron) they rejoined No 29 Squadron in July 1942, and in just a few weeks they destroyed three enemy bombers and damaged three more.

In October 1942 the Braham-Gregory team shot down a Junkers 88 and a Dornier 217. In the following month, Braham was promoted and given command of No 141 Squadron, beginning night intruder operations in June 1943. On his first such mission, on 14 June, he shot down a Messerschmitt 110, and by the end of September he had brought his score to twenty enemy aircraft destroyed, nineteen of them at night. He was now level with John Cunningham, but his second operational tour was at an end and it was not until February 1944 that he was again permitted to fly operationally, and then only on a limited basis, as Wing Commander (Night Operations) at HQ No 2 Group.

Changing his tactics, Braham made six low-level daylight intruder sorties into occupied Europe in March and April 1944, and on five of these trips he destroyed seven enemy aircraft. On the first sortie on 5 March (he was now flying a Mosquito, borrowed from No 305 Squadron at Lasham) he shot down a Heinkel 177, the biggest aircraft he had so far destroyed. His run of luck came to an end on 25 June 1944, when, flying a No 21 Squadron Mosquito, he was hit by flak and had to make a forced landing on a sandbar near Ringkobing, Denmark. He spent the rest of the war in prison camp, as did his Australian navigator, Flight Lieutenant Don Walsh. Braham's score at the time of his capture was 29 confirmed kills, making him the leading RAF night-fighter pilot. He was also the first RAF pilot ever to be awarded three DSOs and three DFCs.

Bob Braham never received any of the publicity accorded to John Cunningham (a fact for which he was probably grateful) but there were other night-fighter pilots who achieved notable successes and who remained almost entirely unknown outside the Service, at least until long after the war. One of them was Flight Lieutenant George Esmond Jamieson, a young New Zealand pilot who, on the night of 29 July 1944, set up an Allied record by destroying four enemy aircraft in one night. He was flying a Mosquito of No 488 RNZAF Squadron on patrol over Normandy, and his navigator was Flying Officer Norman Crookes. Jamieson's combat report tells part of the story:

'I was patrolling the Coutance–St Lo area when I saw an unidentified aircraft approaching head-on at 5,000 feet height. Against the dawn I saw that it was a Junkers 88 and as I turned hard to port I followed him as he skimmed through the cloud tops. I closed to 300 yards and there was a series of explosions from the ground caused by the Junkers dropping his bombs as he tried to get away. I gave two short bursts as we came to the next clear patch, and after a fire in the port engine and fuselage the Ju 88 went down through the clouds vertically, hitting the ground near Caen.'

As Jamieson looked down at the debris of the Ju 88, Norman Crookes detected another aircraft on his radar and steered the pilot towards it. As he closed in, the unexpected happened: yet another Junkers suddenly burst out of the cloud, dead ahead of the Mosquito. The German pilot saw the danger and went into a diving turn, trying to regain the shelter of the clouds, but he was too late. Jamieson opened fire from a range of 350 yards, and flames were soon streaming back from the Junkers' starboard engine. The aircraft fell through the cloud layer, burning fiercely, and plunged into the ground.

'Almost immediately I obtained a brief visual on an aircraft crossing from port to starboard some 5,000 feet away and identified as a Ju 88. My navigator confirmed this and took over on his "box of tricks", keeping me behind the enemy aircraft, which was now taking violent evasive action and at the same time jamming our equipment. When we were down to almost treetop height I regained the visual at only 250 yards, opening fire immediately and causing the Junkers to pull up almost vertically, turning to port with sparks and debris falling away. The Ju eventually stalled and dived into a four-acre field where it exploded. This was near Lisieux and as the time was now 0515 hours I climbed back to 5,000 feet and requested control to vector me back to any activity, as I had already observed further anti-aircraft fire through the clouds ahead.'

The anti-aircraft fire, Jamieson soon established, was directed at a Dornier 217, whose pilot spotted the Mosquito as it closed in and began a series of violent evasive manoeuvres. Just as the Dornier was about to plunge into cloud, Jamieson opened fire and saw his shells bursting on the enemy's fuselage. The Dornier went down in flames, its rear gunner continuing to fire back almost until the bomber hit the ground.

Jamieson returned to New Zealand shortly after his exploit. His score was eleven enemy aircraft destroyed, one probably destroyed and two damaged, all of them at night or in weather conditions so bad that day fighters were unable to intercept. Eight of the enemy bombers had been shot down while trying to attack Allied forces in Normandy, and the four kills of 29 July were all achieved within twenty minutes.

One Mosquito night-fighter/intruder team that enjoyed considerable success was Flight Lieutenant James Benson and Squadron Leader Lewis Brandon (navigator) of No 157 Squadron. Together, they scored seven confirmed kills, with a number of claims for aircraft probably destroyed and damaged, and also destroyed six V-1 flying bombs in the summer of 1944. On the night of 11/12 September 1944, while flying bomber support operations with No 100 (Countermeasures) Group, they were flying over the island of Seeland, off the south-east coast of Denmark, when Brandon picked up a transmission from an enemy night-fighter radar. A few moments later, he made contact with the suspect aircraft on his AI radar and steered Benson towards it. In the clear moonlight, the enemy was identified as a Junkers 188; it was flying in broad circles, apparently orbiting a German radio beacon.

Benson slid in astern of the 188 and fired a burst into it, seeing his 20-mm shells strike home on the night-fighter's starboard wing root. The 188 lost speed rapidly, its starboard engine catching fire, and Benson had to pull up sharply to avoid a collision. The 188 was last seen plunging earthwards, streaming flames. At that moment, Brandon picked up another contact. It was a second Ju 188, and it had probably been engaged in a night-fighting exercise with the first. Benson closed in rapidly and gave the Junkers a two-second burst; bright flames streamed back from the enemy's ruptured fuel tanks and it dropped away towards the Danish coast, shedding great chunks of wreckage. The Mosquito sped through the cloud of smoke and debris that the Junkers left in its wake; when Benson and Brandon returned to base they found their aircraft smothered in oil and scarred by pieces of flying metal.

The team's last air combat occurred on the night of 5/6 January 1945, over northern Germany. They had been following a contact which, disappointingly, turned out to be a Lancaster bomber when Brandon suddenly picked up another trace on his radar screen. Whatever the strange aircraft was, it proved very hard to catch, climbing fast towards Hannover. Benson finally caught it at a range of half a mile over the burning city and identified it as a Heinkel 219, a fast, twin-engined fighter with a formidable armament, easily recognisable because of its twin fins and array of radar aerials.

Benson crept up behind the enemy aircraft and opened fire at 200 yards, hitting the Heinkel's engines. Large pieces broke off and it went down in a steep dive, with the Mosquito following. At 6,000 feet the enemy night-fighter entered a steep climb up to 12,000 feet, where it heeled over and dived almost vertically to the ground. The Mosquito crew saw it blow up. Later, it was learned that the Heinkel 219 was fitted with ejection seats, the first aircraft in the world to use them. From the aircraft's erratic behaviour after its initial dive, it seemed likely that the crew of this particular He 219 had ejected from their stricken machine.

The story of the He 219 – which could have wrought havoc with the RAF's night bombers had it been available in sufficient numbers – was typical of the muddled thinking and erratic policies that dogged Germany's fighter aircraft industry in the later years of the war. And yet the *Luftwaffe*'s night-fighter arm, after a slow beginning, had soon shown potential as an effective counter-force against Bomber Command's growing offensive.

From the moment of his appointment in 1940, General Josef Kammhuber strove to weld the German night defences into as efficient an organisation as his resources would permit. He was the architect of the *Himmelbett* system, a network of overlapping air defence zones stretching from north to south across the length of occupied Europe, and was a firm advocate of night intruder operations as a means of inflicting the maximum possible damage on Bomber Command over its own territory. The intruder offensive against the RAF's bomber bases began on a limited scale in the summer of 1941 and enjoyed some success, being undertaken mainly by the Junkers 88s of I/NJG 2, based at Gilze-Rijen, but several very experienced German crews were also lost, and in October 1941 Adolf Hitler called a personal halt to operations of this kind.

Apart from the *Luftwaffe*'s losses, his standpoint was that the German people wanted to see enemy bombers brought down over the territory they were attacking: it was good for morale. And by the middle of 1942, there was no doubt that the German night-fighter crews – still without the benefit of AI radar – were becoming more proficient. In the early hours of 3 June 1941, the first RAF bomber to be destroyed over Berlin – a Short Stirling – was shot down by Sergeant Kalinowski and Sergeant Zwickl, the crew of a Messerschmitt 110, and on 28 June four RAF bombers were shot down in quick succession over Hamburg by First Lieutenant Eckardt of II/NJG 1.

Meanwhile, on his own initiative, Kammhuber had asked the Telefunken Company if they could produce an airborne AI radar. Telefunken obliged, and in July 1941 a prototype set, named *Lichtenstein*, was installed in a Messerschmitt 110 based at Leeuwarden, Holland. On 9 August, this aircraft, crewed by First Lieutenant Ludwig Becker and Sergeant Josef Staub, intercepted a Wellington bomber with the aid of *Lichtenstein* and shot it down. Despite this success, Kammhuber had to maintain constant pressure to have his night-fighters fitted with AI radar, and it was not until early in 1942 that *Lichtenstein*-equipped aircraft reached the *Nachtjagdgeschwader* (Night Fighter Wings) in any numbers. Once they did, the effectiveness of the German night-fighter force increased immeasurably, and some pilots began to achieve quite remarkable scores. One of them was Captain Werner Streib, commanding I/NJG 1 at Venlo, who – accompanied by his observer, Corporal Lingen – destroyed his first bomber, a Whitley, on the night of 20/21 July 1940 while flying an Me 110. In August Streib destroyed three more RAF bombers, and on the night of 1/2 October he intercepted and destroyed three Wellingtons inside forty minutes.

Streib went on to gain 66 victories, and for a long time he was Germany's top-scoring night-fighter pilot; but close behind him came Lieutenant Helmut Lent, a veteran Me 110 pilot who had fought over Poland, Norway and in the defence of Germany against the early (and disastrous) daylight raids on the north German ports by RAF Bomber Command. On 1 November, 1941, Lent formed a new night-fighter *Gruppe,* II/NJG 2; his squadron commanders were Captain Rudolf Schönert, Captain Prince Lippe-Weissenfeld, and Captain Ludwig Becker. All of them went on to achieve exceptional night-fighting scores. Helmut Lent destroyed 102 aircraft at night and eight by day before his death in a flying accident on 7 October 1944; Lippe-Weissenfeld got 56 before his death in action on 12 March 1944; and Becker had 46 kills when he too was shot down, in February 1943.

Colonel Helmut Lent, the second-ranking German night fighter ace, was awarded the Third Reich's highest decoration, the Oak Leaves with Swords and Diamonds. So was the top-scorer, Major Heinz-Wolfgang Schnaufer, who gained an incredible 121 victories in the night sky over Germany. Schnaufer, scored many multiple kills; on 25 May 1944, for example, he shot down five Lancasters in a quarter of an hour, and on 21 February 1945 he destroyed two Lancasters in the early morning and seven more after nightfall, a total of nine in a single day. Schnaufer was a quite exceptional pilot, and his achievement was all the more noteworthy in that he gained his victories in just 164 combat sorties.

By the spring of 1943, Kammhuber had five *Geschwader* (Wings) and 400 twin-engined fighters under his command on bases stretching from Holland to the Mediterranean. However, he was the first to realise that 400 night-fighters were not enough to counter the great armadas of four-engined bombers which were beginning to make deeper inroads into Germany night after night, and he consequently proposed a major extension of the *Himmelbett* air defence system, with eighteen night-fighter *Geschwader* covering the whole of Germany. The aircraft would be fitted with improved AI equipment and the ground radar network would also be modernised.

Kammhuber pushed relentlessly for the expansion of his night-fighter force and it was his undoing. Nothing could convince Hitler that the *Luftwaffe*'s night-fighters were not already destroying enough enemy bombers to cripple the RAF's night offensive. Kammhuber rapidly began to fall from favour, and his cause was not helped when, during a series of heavy attacks on Hamburg in July 1943, Bomber Command rendered the *Himmelbett* radar system virtually impotent by the use of 'window', bundles of tinfoil strips cut to the wavelength of the enemy warning radar and dropped from attacking aircraft to confuse the defences. In November 1943, Kammhuber was relieved of his appointment as commander of the German night-fighter force.

The paralysing of the *Himmelbett* system led to the evolution of new tactics, stemming from a proposal made by a Colonel von Lossberg of the General Staff. He recommended that night-fighters be released from the confines of the *Himmelbett* zones, where their movements were too restricted and susceptible to radar jamming, and instead mix freely with the bomber stream, the fighter pilots making visual attacks. The idea was approved, and it was decided as a first step to increase the strength of *Jagdgeschwader* 300, formed a month earlier under the command of Major Hajo Herrmann, himself a fighter ace. This was the pioneer *Wilde Sau* (Wild Boar) unit; equipped with single-engined fighters, its task was to patrol directly over German targets, the pilots endeavouring to pick out enemy bombers in the glare of searchlights and fires.

The idea was quickly adopted by other night-fighter units, including NJG 1, and it achieved considerable success – although at great risk to the attacking fighters, which had to contend with German flak as well as defensive fire from the RAF bombers. The following combat report, one of the few to survive the wholesale destruction of *Luftwaffe* records that took place in the final days of the war, was made by Lieutenant Musset of 5/NJG 1. His radio operator was Corporal Hafner.

'At 23.47 hours on 17.8.43 I took off from Berlin on a *Wilde Sau* operation. From the Berlin area I observed enemy activity to the north. I promptly flew in that direction and positioned myself at a height of 14,000 feet over the enemy's target, Peenemünde [Germany's secret rocket weapons research establishment, hit by 597 RAF heavy bombers that night – author]. Against the glow of the burning target I saw from above numerous enemy aircraft flying over it in close formations of seven or eight.

'I went down and placed myself at 11,000 feet behind one enemy formation. At 01.42 I attacked one of the enemy with two bursts of fire from directly astern, registering good strikes on the port inboard engine, which at once caught fire. E/A (enemy aircraft) tipped over to its left and went down. Enemy counter-fire from rear gunner was ineffective. Owing to an immediate second engagement I could only follow E/A's decsent on fire as far as a layer of mist.

'I make four claims, as follows:

1. Attack at 01.45 on a four-engined E/A at 8,500 feet from astern and range 30–40 yards. E/A at once burned brightly in both wings and fuselage. I observed it until it crashed in flames at 01.47.
2. At 01.50 I was in position to attack another E/A from slightly above, starboard astern and range 60–70 yards. Strikes were seen in starboard wing, and E/A blew up. I observed burning fragments hit the ground at 01.52.
3. At 01.57 I attacked another four-engined E/A at 6,000 feet from 100 yards astern. Burning brightly in both wings and fuselage it went into a vertical dive. After its crash I saw the wreckage burning at 01.58. Heavy counter-fire from near gunner scored hits in both wings of our own aircraft.
4. At 01.59 I was ready to attack again. E/A took strong evasive action by weaving. While it was in a left-hand turn, however, I got in a burst from port astern and range 40–50 yards, which set the port wing on fire. E/A plunged to the ground burning brightly, and I observed the crash at 02.01. Enemy counter-fire from rear gunner was ineffective.

'A few minutes later I attacked another E/A which took violent evasive action by weaving. On the first attack my cannon went out of action owing to burst barrels. I then made three further attacks with MG and observed good strikes on the starboard wing without, however, setting it on fire. Owing to heavy counter-fire from enemy rear-gunner I suffered hits in my own port engine. At the same time I came under fire from enemy aircraft on the starboard beam, which wounded radio operator in the left shoulder and set my Me 110's port engine on fire. Thereupon I broke off the action, cut my engine and flew westwards away from the target area. No radio contact with the ground could be established, and ES-signals were also unavailing. As I was constantly losing height, at 6,000 feet I gave the order to bale out.

'As I did so I struck the tail unit with both legs, thereby breaking my right thigh and left shin-bone. After normal landings by parachute my radio operator and I were taken to the reserve military hospital at Güstrow.

At 02.50 the Me 110 crashed on the northern perimeter of Güstrow.'

Four heavy bombers, each with a crew of seven, destroyed in fifteen minutes, together with one probably destroyed and one damaged! And such engagements were by no means uncommon during the night battle over Germany. That night, forty RAF bombers failed to return from Peenemünde. The loss would undoubtedly have been higher, had it not been for a diversionary effort by a small force of RAF Mosquitos, which dropped flares over Berlin and duped the defences into believing that this was the objective. The result was that 148 *Wilde Sau* fighters patrolled over the capital for the best part of an hour without sighting a single enemy aircraft.

While *Wilde Sau* operations continued, Telefunken had been hard at work developing a new AI radar that would not be susceptible to 'window' jamming. In October 1943 the night-fighter units began to receive the new *Lichtenstein* SN-2 AI radar, which was free from both electronic and 'window' jamming. It had a maximum range of four miles and a minimum range of 450 yards, and it was not long before some night-fighter crews began to register a formidable number of successes with its help. In the autumn of 1943 two more homing devices were also developed for use by night-fighters, the *Naxos* Z and the *Flensburg*. The former enabled the fighters to home on transmissions from the RAF's H2S blind bombing radar, and the latter was designed to lock on to radiations from the 'Monica' tail warning radar carried by the bombers.

In the summer of 1943 the German night-fighters also began to receive a new type of armament, which was to prove horribly effective. Devised by a sergeant armourer named Paul Mahle and known as *Schräge Musik* (slanting music), it involved the mounting of two 20-mm cannon, their muzzles pointing upwards at a fixed angle, on a wooden platform in the upper fuselage of a night-fighter. This arrangement enabled the fighter to take advantage of a bomber's blind spot and attack it from directly below with the aid of a reflector sight mounted in the cockpit roof.

Schräge Musik was used for the first time on the night of 17/18 August 1943, when two crews of II/NJG 5 destroyed six RAF bombers in the space of 30 minutes. The German airmen reported that the Halifaxes and Lancasters were extremely vulnerable to this form of attack. The large area of their wings was impossible to miss, and since the wings contained the fuel tanks a relatively short burst was usually enough to set a bomber on fire. Between the night of the Peenemünde raid and 2 October, the crews of II/NJG 5 scored eighteen victories with the aid of *Schräge Musik* for no loss to themselves.

Despite the problems of equipment and organisation that handicapped the German night-fighter force, its success rate reached an unprecedented peak in the spring of 1944. In the course of three big air battles over darkened Germany, Bomber Command suffered crippling losses. On the night of 19/20 February, 78 out of a force of 823 heavy bombers despatched to attack Leipzig failed to return; 72 more were destroyed during an assault on Berlin on 24/25 March; and then, five nights later, came the most catastrophic loss of all, and the greatest triumph for the German night-fighters.

At nightfall on 30 March 1944, 795 heavy bombers set out from their English bases to attack the vital industrial centre and railway junction of Nuremberg. The night was cloudless and calm, and across a great arc of Europe stretching across Holland, Belgium, northern France and north-west Germany the *Luftwaffe* night-fighter crews were at cockpit readiness. At 22.00 reports began to come in of small-scale attacks by Mosquitos on several airfields in Holland and of minelaying operations over the North Sea, but the GOC I Fighter Corps, Major-General Josef Schmid, realised that these were simply diversions and kept his fighters on the ground. Then, at 22.30, the German coastal radar stations detected a major raid building up on the other side of the Channel, and a few minutes later the bomber stream was reported to be heading south-eastwards towards Belgium. At 23.30 Schmid finally ordered his fighters into the air.

This time, instead of carrying out the normal procedure and making several abrupt changes of course to confuse the defences, the bomber stream steered due east for 150 miles after making landfall on the enemy coast, and the night-fighters had no difficulty in locating their targets. The route to Nuremberg was marked by a series of fiery beacons as one heavy bomber after another fell burning from the sky. From all over Germany the night-fighter *Gruppen* converged on the bomber stream, and several pilots scored multiple kills in the running battle that developed. The greatest success was achieved by First Lieutenant Martin Becker of I/NJG 6, who destroyed no fewer than six Halifax bombers in half an hour, between 00.20 and 00.50. Nor was that all: after landing to refuel and rearm, Becker took off again in his Me 110 and shot down a seventh Halifax as it was on its homeward flight.

Other pilots who achieved notable successes that night were First Lieutenant Helmut Schulte of II/NJG 5, who destroyed four heavy bombers; Lieutenant Wilhelm Seuss of IV/NJG 5, who also shot down four; and First Lieutenant Martin Drewes of II/NJG 1, who destroyed three.

For RAF Bomber Command, the cost of the Nuremberg raid was stupendous: 95 bombers failed to return and 71 were damaged. The loss – 11.8 per cent of the attacking force – was the highest ever sustained by the Command. It was the greatest victory achieved by the German night-fighter force during the war – but it was also its last. One by one, the leading German night-fighter pilots were swallowed up in the cauldron of the air war as 1944 wore on; the *Luftwaffe*'s night-fighter resources dwindled steadily through attrition in combat and through Allied bombing. For example, 465 Me 110s, earmarked for night-fighting, were destroyed by bombing in February 1944 alone.

In the first half of 1943, General Kammhuber had pressed strongly for the production of new twin-engined types designed specifically for night-fighting. At the forefront of these was the Heinkel He 219 Uhu (Owl) mentioned earlier in this chapter, the prototype of which had flown in November 1942 after months of delay caused by lack of interest in the German Air Ministry. By April 1943 300 examples had been ordered; Kammhuber wanted 2,000, but in the event only 294 were built before the end of the war. Formidably armed with six 20-mm cannon and equipped with the latest AI radar, the He 219 would undoubtedly have torn great gaps in Bomber Command's ranks had it been available in quantity. It also had a performance comparable to that of the Mosquito, which the other German night-fighters did not, and therefore could have fought the RAF's intruders on equal terms.

Admittedly, the He 219 suffered from a series of technical troubles in its early development career, but what it might have achieved in action was ably demonstrated on the night of 11/12 June 1943 by Major Werner Streib of I/NJG 1. Flying a pre-production He 219 on operational trials from Venlo, he infiltrated an RAF bomber stream heading for Berlin and shot down five Lancasters in half an hour. The only sour note for Streib sounded when the flaps of the He 219 refused to function and the aircraft over-ran the runway on landing, breaking into three pieces. Streib and his observer escaped without injury.

Werner Streib was one of 30 *Luftwaffe* night-fighter pilots to score 40 or more victories. Between them, they destroyed 1,800 aircraft – the equivalent of 120 RAF bomber squadrons. The two top-scorers have already been mentioned; in third place was Major Prince Sayn-Wittgenstein, with 83 victories, who was killed on 21 January 1944.

Their exploits were largely eclipsed by those of the German day-fighters, who received the lion's share of publicity. But it should never be forgotten that, in the early months of 1944, the German night-fighter force came close to bringing the RAF's night offensive to a standstill.

CHAPTER SIX

The Royal Navy's Aces

Although the first German aircraft to fall on British soil in World War Two was shot down by the Royal Air Force, the first German machine to be destroyed after the outbreak of hostilities in fact fell to the guns of Fleet Air Arm pilots. It happened on 25 September 1939, when a flight of Blackburn Skua fighters from the aircraft carrier HMS *Ark Royal* encountered a Dornier Do 18 reconnaissance flying-boat off the Norwegian coast and sent it crippled into the sea. The British fighters were led by Lieutenant C.L.G. Evans, who was to end the war as the leading Fleet Air Arm ace, with sixteen and a half enemy aircraft to his credit.

The first of the Royal Navy's aces, however, was created during the abortive Norwegian campaign of April 1940. He was Lieutenant Bill Lucy of No 800 Squadron, whose Skuas – together with Sea Gladiators – provided air cover for Fleet Air Arm dive-bombers which were attacking warships operating in support of the German invasion force. On 10 April 1940, Lucy led his Skuas in a dive-bombing attack that sank the German cruiser *Königsberg* in Bergen harbour. Then, during subsequent operations over Norway, he destroyed five enemy bombers in the space of three days. On 14 April, he was engaging a Heinkel 111 bomber when a burst of fire from the German rear gunner found his Skua's petrol tank. The aircraft exploded, killing Lucy and his gunner.

Late in May 1940, before the Norwegian campaign was over, three Skua squadrons – Nos 801, 803 and the recently-formed No 806 – moved to bases in southern England to help cover the evacuation of the British Expeditionary Force from Dunkirk. In addition to the Skuas, No 806 also had a few Blackburn Rocs, the fighter version of the Skua (which was basically a dive-bomber with a secondary fighter role) fitted with a four-gun Boulton Paul turret. During the Dunkirk operations, No 806 Squadron – led by C.L.G. Evans, now a lieutenant-commander – claimed the destruction of two Junkers 88s, one of which was shot down by Evans, and two Me 109s were also claimed by the pilots of No 801 Squadron.

After Dunkirk, a number of Fleet Air Arm pilots were attached to RAF Fighter Command and fought with distinction in the Battle of Britain. The first to become an ace while flying with the RAF was Sub-Lieutenant F. Dawson-Paul, who flew Spitfires with No 64 Squadron and took part in the fierce air fighting over the Channel in July, as the Germans attacked British coastal convoys and tried to draw Fighter Command into battle. During that month, Dawson-Paul destroyed seven enemy aircraft, mostly fighters, and shared in the destruction of a seventh before he too was shot down on the 25th.

Two FAA pilots flew Hurricanes with No 242 Squadron, commanded by Squadron Leader Douglas Bader – the legendary legless pilot who was himself to gain 22½ victories before being shot down over France and taken prisoner in 1941.

They were Sub-Lieutenant R.J. 'Dickie' Cork and Sub-Lieutenant R.E. 'Jimmie' Gardner. The latter destroyed his first enemy aircraft, a Heinkel 111, in July, but it was in the battles of late August and September that he and Cork began to increase their scores. One of the most hectic battles took place on 7 September, when the Germans launched their first big assault on London. Four days later, Dickie Cork wrote:

'We had great fun last Saturday – we ran into about 200–250 German bombers and fighters. The squadron got fourteen – my share of the bag was one Dornier bomber and a Messerschmitt 110 – brings my total to five. Unfortunately or not, I don't know, I was flying in the first section with the CO and before we knew where we were we found ourselves in the middle of all this mass. Every way you turned all you could see were German machines – and was there some lead flying about the sky! Anyway we stuck together and got out of it without injury except a few scratches from glass and odd bits of bullets, but you should have seen our machines – absolutely full of holes and they couldn't even make one whole aircraft out of what was left.'

By the end of October Cork had added a 'probable' to his score, while Gardner had gained four kills and one probable. Both were to see considerable action later in the war, as was another FAA pilot, Sub-Lieutenant D.M. Jeram. He flew Hurricanes with No 213 Squadron, claiming two bombers and two Messerschmitt 110s in August. One other FAA pilot, Sub-Lieutenant A.G. Blake, destroyed six and a half enemy aircraft while flying Spitfires with No 19 Squadron in the Battle of Britain; he shot down two Me 109s on each of his last two combats, but was then shot down and killed also.

Meanwhile, in the Mediterranean, the British Fleet had been subjected to repeated attacks by Italian aircraft following Italy's declaration of war in June 1940. The main target was the aircraft carrier HMS *Eagle*, which then only had Swordfish torpedo-bombers on board, but in July four Sea Gladiators were picked up from Malta and these were formed into a fighter flight within No 813 Squadron. The flight was led by Commander C.L. Keighley-Peach, *Eagle's* Commander Flying and the only man on the carrier with fighter experience. While on Malta he trained two Swordfish pilots, Lieutenant L.K. Keith and Lieutenant A.N. Young, to fly the Gladiators. In July and August 1940 these three destroyed eleven Italian aircraft, mainly Savoia SM79 bombers, without loss to themselves. Six of these aircraft were claimed by Keighley-Peach, who was wounded in the leg during one combat.

Towards the end of August 1940, the Royal Navy's striking force in the Mediterranean received a powerful addition in the shape of the carrier HMS *Illustrious*. In addition to her two Swordfish squadrons, she carried No 806 Squadron, which after the Dunkirk operation had become the first Fleet Air Arm unit to exchange its Skuas and Rocs for the Fairey Fulmar, the Navy's new monoplane fighter. The Fulmar was fitted with eight Browning .303 machine-guns, and although its top speed of 270 mph made it a good deal slower than contemporary land-based fighters such as the Hurricane, it was a distinct improvement on the Sea Gladiator and Skua. Fourteen FAA squadrons were eventually equipped with it.

For the first time, thanks to the Fulmars, Admiral Cunningham, the C-in-C Mediterranean Fleet, now had a means of countering the Italian high-level attacks and the reconnaissance aircraft that shadowed his warships. The pilots of No 806 Squadron soon began to chalk up an increasing number of kills against the Cant Z501 flying boats and Z506B floatplanes, as well as against the SM79 bombers. After some two months of operations, the squadron's tally stood at twenty enemy aircraft destroyed. Three pilots particularly distinguished themselves; Lieutenant W.L. Barnes became an ace with five victories, while several more Italian aircraft were shot down by Lieutenant-Commander Evans and Sub-Lieutenant S.G. Orr. Evans was to become the leading Fleet Air Arm ace with sixteen and a half kills, followed by Dickie Cork with thirteen and Orr with twelve.

On 10 January 1941, Stuka dive-bombers of the *Luftwaffe*, operating from bases in Sicily, carried out heavy attacks on HMS *Illustrious*. The Fulmars of No 806 Squadron shot down five of the attackers and also two SM79 torpedo-bombers, but *Illustrious* was badly damaged and limped into Malta for repairs.

Her place was taken by HMS *Ark Royal*, which had two Fulmar squadrons, Nos 807 and 808. In March she was joined by HMS *Formidable*, with the Fulmars of No 803 Squadron, and in April she also embarked No 806 Squadron, whose Fulmars had been land-based on Malta while HMS *Illustrious* was undergoing repair. On 8 May 1941, the carriers were subjected to heavy air attacks while escorting a convoy carrying tanks and aircraft to Alexandria, and in a day of severe fighting the Fulmar pilots accounted for eleven enemy aircraft. Two Ju 87 Stukas were shot down by Lieutenant Jimmie Gardner, who had fought with No 242 Squadron; his own aircraft was hit and he crash-landed on *Ark Royal*'s deck. Six more enemy aircraft were claimed by No 803 Squadron; one Heinkel 111 was destroyed by Lieutenant J.M. Bruen, who had already shared in a number of victories while flying Skuas.

In May 1941, with the battle for Greece lost and the Allied forces withdrawn to Crete, No 805 Squadron of the Fleet Air

Arm was hurriedly sent to the island to provide air defence. Commanded by Lieutenant-Commander A.C. Black, DSC, the unit was equipped with a mixed collection of aircraft – mostly Fulmars, but also a handful of American-built Brewster Buffalos and a few Sea Gladiators. In the event, most of these aircraft were destroyed on the ground by strafing German fighters before they had a chance to fire their guns in anger. The surviving pilots attached themselves to the RAF's two Hurricane squadrons on Crete, Nos 33 and 80. On 16 May three Hurricanes flown by Fleet Air Arm pilots tackled a formation of 30 Junkers 88s escorted by fifteen Messerschmitt 109s; two of the British fighters were shot down almost immediately, but the surviving pilot, Lieutenant A.R. Ramsay, managed to destroy two of the enemy before he was forced to break off the fight.

In September 1941, Lieutenant-Commander Alan Black took command of Nos 803 and 806 Squadrons, which had been transferred from HMS *Formidable* – damaged by air attack – and formed into a composite fighter unit in the Western Desert, together with No 805 Squadron. Nos 803 and 806 exchanged their Fulmars for Hurricanes, while No 805, which had lost all its equipment in Crete, was now flying Grumman Martlets, the Royal Navy's version of the US Navy's stocky little Wildcat fighter. The Navy pilots established close co-operation with the RAF, escorting Blenheims and Baltimores during raids on Rommel's supply lines and flying offensive fighter sweeps. It was during one of these escort missions, on 28 September, that the composite unit scored its first kill when one of the Martlet pilots, Sub-Lieutenant W.M. Walsh, shot down an Italian Fiat G.50 fighter.

On 20 November, Lieutenant-Commander Black was leading a flight of Hurricanes at 8,000 feet, with an RAF Tomahawk squadron above, when they ran into a formation of twelve Ju 87s escorted by twice as many Me 109s. In the ensuing battle, one FAA pilot, Sub-Lieutenant P.N. Charlton, shot down three Stukas before a burst from an Me 109 forced him to take to his parachute. He was later awarded a DFC by the RAF. His was the only aircraft lost, in exchange for seven Ju 87s destroyed. As the British aircraft broke off the combat and returned to base, short of fuel, the last thing Black saw – as he said later – was 'two Messerschmitts knocking hell out of a third'.

The Fleet Air Arm fighter pilots fought their most desperate air battles in the Mediterranean in August 1942, when four aircraft carriers with eight fighter squadrons escorted a large convoy fighting its way through to the besieged island of Malta. The armada sailed from Gibraltar on 9 August, but the following day the carrier HMS *Eagle* was torpedoed and sunk, taking most of the aircraft of her two fighter squadrons with her.

On 11 August, a Junkers 88 was sighted shadowing the convoy. Lieutenant Dickie Cork, flying a Sea Hurricane of No 880 Squadron from HMS *Indomitable*, intercepted it and shot it down. The next day the convoy, now well within the range of enemy airfields, was subjected to a series of very heavy attacks in which HMS *Indomitable*'s two Sea Hurricane squadrons gave a particularly good account of themselves. No 800 Squadron claimed four and a half Ju 87s, three Ju 88s, an SM84, an SM79 and an Me 109; individual claims were three and a half for Sub-Lieutenant A.J. Thompson and two and a half each for Lieutenant-Commander J.M. Bruen and Sub-Lieutenant B. Ritchie. No 880 Squadron's score was two Ju 88s, two SM79s, a Cant Z1007, an Me 110, a Macchi 202 and half a Ju 87. No fewer than five of these aircraft were destroyed by Lieutenant Dickie Cork in the course of three sorties, an exploit that earned him a DSO. In three days of fighting the FAA fighters claimed 38 confirmed kills for the loss of thirteen of their own number, some of which ditched after running out of fuel.

The Fleet Air Arm's next major operations in the Mediterranean were flown in support of Operation Torch, the Allied landings in North Africa in November 1942. The operations were supported by seven British carriers, their fighter squadrons operating Sea Hurricanes, Martlets and – for the first time – Seafires, the navalised version of the Spitfire. Soon after the task forces entered the Mediterranean, a Vichy French Potez 63 reconnaissance aircraft flew overhead at 10,000 feet; it was intercepted by a patrol of Martlets of No 888 Squadron, HMS *Formidable*, and shot down in flames by Lieutenant D.M. Jeram, the former Battle of Britain pilot.

On 8 November, the day the landings began, considerable opposition was encountered from Vichy fighters, mostly Dewoitine D.520s, which inflicted considerable damage on the FAA's Fairey Albacore bombers. On an early sortie, a D.520 was shot down by Lieutenant G.C. Baldwin; it was the first kill scored by a Seafire. Later, five more D.520s were claimed by the Sea Hurricanes of No 800 Squadron, two being shot down by Sub-Lieutenant Mike Crosley and one each by Sub-Lieutenant Ritchie, Sub-Lieutenant R.C. Thompson and Lieutenant-Commander Bruen.

One other carrier pilot who took part in Operation Torch deserves a mention. He was Captain R.C. Hay of the Royal Marines, who had been in the Mediterranean since January 1941 with No 807 Squadron, flying Fulmars. During the North African landings Hay flew Fulmars in the reconnaissance role. He had three victories to his credit.

In the Atlantic, the majority of Fleet Air Arm fighter squadrons had re-equipped with Martlets and Sea Hurricanes by the summer of 1941. The first victory by a Sea Hurricane came on 21 July that year, when Lieutenant-Commander F.E.C. Judd (later to lose his life during the Malta convoy battle of August 1942) and Sub-Lieutenant R.B. Howarth of No 880 Squadron intercepted a Dornier 18 off northern Norway and shot it down. In general, however, combat in the Atlantic was sporadic, although the FAA fighters occasionally managed to shoot down an enemy reconnaissance aircraft.

It was a different story early in 1945, when the Royal Navy's carrier task forces sailed to join their American counterparts in the Pacific War. *En route* from Ceylon to Australia, the British carrier aircraft struck hard at the Japanese oil refineries in Sumatra. The FAA fighter squadrons were equipped with American-built Hellcats and Corsairs, and British Seafires and Fireflies. Early in the operation, a Japanese Kawasaki Ki 45 reconnaissance aircraft was shot down by Lieutenant P.S. Cole of No 1830 Squadron, flying a Corsair, and a similar aircraft was destroyed a few minutes later by a Hellcat of No 1839 Squadron. In the air battle that developed during the attack on the refineries, fourteen enemy aircraft were destroyed in air combat; Sub-Lieutenant A. French of No 1836 Squadron shot down two of them, as did Major R.C. Hay of the Royal Marines, the Air Co-ordinator on HMS *Victorious*. Hay was now an ace, with five victories. Two Oscar fighters were also shot down by a young Canadian, Sub-Lieutenant D.J. Sheppard, a Corsair pilot who was also to become an ace with five victories before the war's end.

The British Pacific Fleet, or Task Force 57 as it was known, went into action in the Pacific in March 1945. On 1 April, during the Okinawa landings, Sub-Lieutenant R. Reynolds of No 894 Squadron, who had already shot down two Blohm und Voss Bv 138 flying-boats over the Atlantic, became an ace when he shot down three Zero fighters in his Seafire. There was heavy action on 6 April, the FAA squadrons claiming the destruction of six enemy aircraft, and again on the 11th and 12th, when eight Japanese aircraft were destroyed. Sub-Lieutenant W.M. Foster and Sub-Lieutenant Fenwick-Smith got two each. On the following day the Fireflies of No 1770 Squadron intercepted a number of Mitsubishi Ki 51 aircraft on a *Kamikaze* suicide mission, Lieutenant W. Thompson and Sub-Lieutenant J.R. Stott claiming two each. Another pilot to score a multiple victory was Lieutenant D.G. Jenkins, who shot down two Zeros on 17 April.

Although the Allies enjoyed air supremacy in the Pacific, there was every indication that the Japanese would continue fighting fanatically to defend their homeland. No-one, at this juncture, could envisage how suddenly, and how dramatically, a formidable enemy would be brought to his knees.

CHAPTER SEVEN

The Fighting Warhawks

For the first year of the war in the Far East, following the Japanese attack on the US Naval base at Pearl Harbor, there was no doubt at all that the Mitsubishi A6M Zero was the best fighter in the theatre, superior on almost every count – the exception being perhaps structural strength – to the types pitted against it by the Allies. It was certainly superior to the standard first-line American fighter of the day, the Curtiss P-40B Warhawk – and yet, in the hands of skilled pilots, the P-40 could give an excellent account of itself, and in some areas was to bear the brunt of air fighting for much of the Far East war.

The P-40 was in action against the Japanese from the very beginning. On 7 December 1941, half a dozen aircraft of the 47th Pursuit Squadron managed to get airborne from Wheeler Field, Hawaii, as the Japanese were attacking the Pearl Harbor base, and in the ensuing air combat they brought down twelve enemy aircraft before they were overwhelmed. Leading the American scorers on this fateful day was Lieutenant George S. Welch, who destroyed four Japanese aircraft, and his friend Lieutenant Ken Taylor, who got two. George Welch later went on to score a total of sixteen victories in the Pacific War; he survived combat only to be killed on 11 October 1954, while testing a North American F-100 Super Sabre jet fighter.

The first P-40 pilots to engage the enemy on a serious scale, however, did not belong to the US Army Air Corps. The area in which they fought was Burma, and they were members of an extraordinary group of mercenaries called the American Volunteer Group, and their expertise was to cost the Japanese dearly.

On the same day that Pearl Harbor was attacked, Japanese forces landed in Thailand and on the north-east coast of Malaya. Next on the list was Burma, which had to be secured before Japan could launch an offensive against the real prize in south-east Asia: India.

As far as the Japanese were aware, the responsibility for the air defence of Burma rested on a single RAF fighter squadron: No 67, which was equipped with American-built Brewster Buffalo fighters. The tubby little Buffalo had been used with considerable success by Finnish pilots against the Russians during the Winter War of 1939–40, but it was no match against the Zero, as the RAF and RAAF squadrons using it in Malaya were already finding out to their cost.

What the Japanese did not know was that the sixteen Buffalos defending the Burmese capital of Rangoon had been joined by twenty-one Curtiss P-40Bs of the American Volunteer Group's 3rd Pursuit Squadron, and that as a consequence their planned air attacks on Burma would prove to be far more costly than they had anticipated.

The origins of the American Volunteer Group went back to 1937, when a retired US Army Air Corps officer named Claire Chennault arrived in China to carry out an appraisal of the Chinese Air Force at the request of Chiang Kai-shek's government. Chennault was appalled by the shortcomings he found, in terms of both pilot and equipment quality; shortcomings which became only too apparent in July 1937, when Japanese forces invaded Manchuria and began pushing inland along the Yangtse river.

Although the Chinese Air Force had 500 aircraft, only 91 were airworthy and only a handful of pilots were fit to fly them in action. Within weeks, the Japanese had gained complete air superiority, and by October 1937 the Chinese had only twelve airworthy aircraft left. In a desperate bid to save the situation an international air squadron was formed, composed of British, Dutch and American volunteers and armed with a motley collection of aircraft purchased by an American arms dealer. Although the squadron flew many missions during the winter of 1937–8, it was hopelessly outclassed and its operations came to an abrupt end early in 1938, when its base at Hankow was destroyed.

It was the Russians who brought the first real aid to the Chinese. Late in 1937, six Soviet Air Force squadrons – four of fighters and two of bombers – were sent to China, together with 350 advisors. The commander of the Russian contingent was an excellent pilot and combat leader named Stepan Suprun, who had fought on the Republican side in the Spanish Civil War. Operating a mixture of I-15 and I-16 fighters, the Russians went into action early in 1938, fighting hard and continuously until early March, when they were withdrawn for a rest.

Their place was taken by the first batch of Russian-trained Chinese pilots, who were flung into action in the defence of Nanking, but once again they proved no match for the Japanese and they were decimated. For the next two years the Russians continued to supply China with aircraft, and to train Chinese pilots, and the Japanese continued to shoot them out of the sky. On one occasion in 1940, for example, 27 I-15 and I-16 fighters came up to intercept Japanese bombers which, escorted by thirteen Zeros, were attacking Hankow; the Zeros – which had just entered operational service that year and which on this occasion were led by Lieutenant Saburo Shindo and Sub-Lieutenant Ayae Shirane, claimed the destruction of all 27 enemy aircraft in a fight lasting 30 minutes.

Meanwhile, after lengthy negotiations, the US Government had agreed to sell 100 P-40Bs to the Chinese at a cost of nine million dollars. Early in 1941, while the fighters were being crated for delivery, Claire Chennault set about recruiting the volunteers who would fly them. The whole operation went ahead in strict secrecy, recruitment being carried out under cover by the Central Aircraft Manufacturing Company (CAMCO). Pilots were offered generous salaries, plus a bonus of 500 dollars for every Japanese aircraft they shot down.

By the end of June 1941 CAMCO's agents had recruited 100 pilots and 150 ground crew. All were serving US military personnel, working under a one-year CAMCO contract and free to return to their units after service in China with no loss of seniority. The first contingent arrived in Rangoon on 28 July and went to Kyedaw airfield, 170 miles to the north, where they embarked on an intensive training programme.

Inevitably, with spare parts in short supply, the arduous training took its toll of the P-40s, so that by the time of the Japanese attack on 7 December only 55 of the original 100 were serviceable. On 10 December, 34 of these, led by Squadron Leader Robert Sandell, flew to Kunming, near the strategically vital Burma Road, while the other 21, under Squadron Leader Arivs Olson, flew to Mingaladon, near Rangoon, to operate alongside No 67 Squadron RAF.

The first combat with the Japanese came on the morning of 20 December, when ten P-40s of Bob Sandell's 1st Pursuit Squadron were scrambled to intercept a similar number of Mitsubishi Ki 21 Sally* bombers heading for Kunming. The bombers were unescorted and Sandell's pilots destroyed six of them in a matter of minutes. One P-40 failed to return, but its pilot, Ed Rector, made a successful forced landing.

On 23 December the Japanese launched a raid on Rangoon, and this time the bombers were escorted by Nakajima Ki 27 Nate fighters, highly manoeuvrable aircraft with fixed undercarriages. The raid was intercepted by Arivs Olson's 3rd Pursuit Squadron and No 67 Squadron, and a fierce air battle developed over the Burmese capital. Between them the American and British pilots destroyed six bombers and four fighters, but the RAF lost five Buffalos and the AVG four P-40s. Two American pilots baled out and were saved.

On Christmas Day the Japanese mounted a second big attack on Rangoon, with 60 bombers escorted by twenty fighters. The enemy formation split up some distance from the city, one half heading for Mingaladon airfield and the other for Rangoon's docks. This time, the Allied pilots had received plenty of warning of the incoming raid, and while the RAF's Buffalos provided top cover over Rangoon the AVG's thirteen P-40s made contact with the enemy ten miles away. The Americans had the advantage of height, and while one P-40 flight attacked the fighter escort – composed of Zeros on this occasion – the rest tore into the bombers. Within minutes, the Japanese formation had been broken up and dispersed across the sky, and the AVG's first

* In WW2 the Allies allocated code-names to Japanese aircraft. Fighters were given male names, e.g. Nate and Oscar, while bombers, transports and reconnaissance aircraft were given female names such as Sally, Betty and Mavis.

fighter ace had been created. Robert P. 'Duke' Hedman got four bombers and a Zero, Charles Older destroyed four bombers, and three bombers were shot down by Robert T. Smith.

When the battle ended, the Americans had destroyed eighteen bombers and six fighters for the loss of two of their own number – both pilots being saved – while No 67 Squadron claimed twelve.

The Japanese now knew what they were up against, and devised new tactics to combat the Anglo-American force. On 28 December, ten P-40s took off to intercept fifteen Japanese bombers that were heading for Rangoon, but as soon as the P-40s were sighted the Japanese turned round and headed back towards the Thai border. The Americans chased them until, short of fuel, they were forced to land at Moulmein airfield. While the P-40s were refuelling many miles from their home base, ten more Japanese bombers, escorted by twenty Zeros, mounted an attack on Mingaladon. Four P-40s and ten Buffalos tried vainly to break up the raid, but they were beaten off by the fighter escort and the bombers got through to drop their loads on the airfield, causing extensive damage to hangars, fuel dumps and grounded aircraft. They returned on the following day, and once more the Allies' fighters were powerless to stop the bombers inflicting severe damage on the docks area of Rangoon, where large quantities of lend-lease equipment destined for China were destroyed.

In January 1942 the AVG mounted a series of attacks on Japanese airfields in Thailand, but because of the range problem their damaging effect was strictly limited and they were more of a nuisance to the enemy than a serious threat. Then, on 20 January, the whole situation underwent a dramatic change when Japanese forces crossed the Thai frontier and advanced rapidly into southern Burma, pushing on towards Rangoon and overwhelming inferior numbers of British, Burmese and Indian troops. From now on, for the Allied air squadrons in Burma, it was to be a story of endless retreat.

The RAF and the AVG fought on, the RAF having now received a small number of Hawker Hurricanes. In February 1942 the Anglo-American force was concentrated at Mingaladon for the defence of Rangoon. On 7 February, the AVG suffered a sad loss when Squadron Leader Robert Sandell, who had five Japanese aircraft to his credit and who was one of the first AVG aces, was killed while testing a newly-repaired P-40. No-one could tell exactly what happened, but eyewitnesses told how the fighter entered a low-altitude roll and dived into the ground.

Sandell's place was taken by Squadron Leader Robert H. Neale. On 25 February, he led six other pilots to intercept 40 Japanese bombers and twenty Zeros bound for Rangoon. The Americans had plenty of warning, and hit the Japanese from higher altitude, with the sun behind them. In the brief air battle that followed, Neale personally destroyed four bombers and probably destroyed another; his pilots claimed another six enemy aircraft between them. Bob Neale went on to become the American Volunteer Group's top-scoring pilot, with sixteen confirmed victories.

At the end of February 1942 the top-scoring AVG pilot was Squadron Leader Jack Newkirk, with 10½ victories. On 24 March, he was shot and killed by light anti-aircraft fire during a strafing attack at Cheing-Mai. By this time the AVG and RAF fighters had moved to Magwe, some 200 miles from Rangoon, but during the last week in March heavy Japanese bombing led to the evacuation of this base too, the RAF contingent withdrawing to India and the AVG to China. From the beginning of April, flights of P-40s were scattered on airstrips all over south-west China, so that the available aircraft could cover as broad a front as possible. The days of the AVG as a cohesive fighting force were rapidly coming to an end.

Both pilots and equipment were worn out, but they continued to perform their task in support of Chiang Kai-shek's forces, strafing enemy road and rail traffic in northern Burma. On 4 July 1942 the American Volunteer Group ceased to be an independent fighting unit and became part of the newly-activated China Air Task Force; it was commanded, by Claire Chennault, newly promoted to brigadier-general.

With this change in organisation, few of the AVG pilots chose to remain in China. Those who did formed the nucleus of the new 23rd Fighter Group, still flying war-weary P-40s. They included Charles Older, whose score with the AVG was 10½ and who was to increase it to 18½ in later battles; Tex Hill, who gained 12¼ kills with the AVG and whose final score was to reach 18¼; Ed Rector, who survived the war with 10½ victories, 6½ of them gained with the AVG; and Robert Little, who also gained

10½ victories before being killed by ground fire on 22 June 1942. Several other notable pilots joined the 23rd Fighter Group in July 1942. They included Albert J. 'Ajax' Baumler, who had scored six kills while flying for the Republicans in the Spanish Civil War; John Alison, who specialized in night interceptions in his P-40 and who shot down eight aircraft; and Bruce K. Holloway, who destroyed ten enemy aircraft while flying with the 23rd and who became the US Air Force Vice Chief of Staff in the 1960s.

Other former AVG pilots went on to carve out distinguished careers for themselves in other theatres. Foremost among them was Lieutenant-Colonel Gregory 'Pappy' Boyington, the leading United States Marine Corps ace with 28 victories, whose F4U Corsairs of the famous VMF-214 'Black Sheep' blazed a trail of destruction across the Pacific. Boyington scored six of his victories with the AVG. Then there was Colonel James H. Howard, who also destroyed six Japanese aircraft while flying with the AVG and who went on to gain six more victories with the 354th Fighter Group, flying P-51 Mustang escort missions over Germany.

The record of the American Volunteer Group stands unique in the annals of air combat. In just over six months of continual operations, with never more than 79 pilots and 55 aircraft available at any one time, the group positively destroyed 286 enemy aircraft, a record that has never been equalled. How many of their 'probables' failed to get home will never be known. The cost to the Americans was twelve pilots, four of whom vanished without trace in the jungle of the land they had fought so hard to defend.

In the Philippines, the Army Air Corps' P-40 squadrons suffered appalling losses from the first day of the Pacific war. The islands were defended by five USAAC P-40 squadrons totalling about 90 aircraft; one-third of this force was wiped out on the ground on the first day of the Japanese attack. Fifteen more P-40s were lost in air combat on 10 December, victims of the highly skilled Zero pilots of the Imperial Japanese Navy.

One of the USAAC P-40 units in the thick of the fighting was the 17th Pursuit Squadron, whose P-40s were based at Del Carmen alongside those of the 34th Pursuit Squadron. The 17th Squadron's commander was Lieutenant Boyd D. Wagner, who on 11 December was leading a flight of P-40s on patrol north of Aparri when they were attacked by five Zeros. In two days of air fighting Wagner had learned how to cope with the highly manoeuvrable Japanese fighters. Now, as two Zeros dived on him, he waited until they were in firing range and then suddenly throttled back. Taken by surprise, the Zero pilots shot past his aircraft. Wagner opened the throttle again, quickly caught up with them in the dive and shot both of them down. A week later, on 18 December, Wagner destroyed three more enemy aircraft to become the first US Army Air Corps ace of World War Two. A few days later he was almost blinded when a cannon shell exploded in his cockpit, filling his eyes full of perspex splinters, but he brought his aircraft home and recovered to fly P-40s and P-39s in New Guinea, raising his score to eight. He was killed in a flying accident later in the war.

In February 1942, with the battle for the Philippines lost and their aircraft destroyed, the surviving P-40 pilots evacuated to Australia, where they joined the 49th Fighter Group at Darwin in time to provide the principal fighter defence of the vital northern Australian port. The 49th was equipped with a more modern variant of the Warhawk, the P-40E, and as the Japanese stepped up their air attacks on Darwin in the spring and summer of 1942 a number of American pilots became aces.

Lieutenant John D. Landers delivered a new P-40 to Darwin on 3 April and was in action the next day, shooting down an enemy bomber. Almost immediately afterwards, he was pounced on by several Zeros, who shot his P-40 full of holes. He dived away and shook them off, then climbed over Melville Island in the hope of picking off any Japanese stragglers returning from the battle over Darwin. A while later, three Zeros passed directly under him and he dived on them, shooting one down. They were the first of six victories Landers was to score during his tour with the 49th.

Lieutenant James B. Morehead had already destroyed two Ki 21 Sally bombers over Java before joining the 49th FG in March 1942. On 29 April 1942, ANZAC Day, the Japanese launched a major attack on Darwin and all three squadrons of the 49th Group were scrambled to intercept the incoming bombers and their fighter escort. Morehead, leading the 8th Squadron, shot down three Mitsubishi G4M Betty bombers, closing right in to make certain of his kills and braving very heavy return fire. His P-40 was hit by 39 machine-gun bullets and two cannon shells, which damaged it so badly that Morehead had to make

Gloster Gladiator biplane fighters of No 72 Squadron pictured before the war. Although outclassed, the Gladiator fought with distinction in Norway, France and the Middle East.

Hawker Hurricane Mk 1 fighters in echelon formation.

Above left: The graceful lines of the Supermarine Spitfire. This famous aircraft was the mount of most of the RAF's aces.
Above right: Flying Officer J.E. 'Cobber' Kain, the New Zealander who was the RAF's top-scoring pilot in the Battle of France.

Photo-reconnaissance aircraft were early victims in the Battle of France. This picture shows the wreck of a Dornier 17.

Heinkel He 111 bomber destroyed by French fighters in the Battle of France.

A French Horane 406 fighter seen alongside a Belgian Air Force Fairey Battle. The Morane was outclassed by the Messerschmitt 109.

Most of the French aces flew the excellent Curtiss Hawk, which was manoeuvrable but under-armed.

RAF Hurricanes seen during a simulated gas attack on a French airfield
during the 'Phoney War' period.

RAF Spitfire pilots relaxing between sorties at Manston, Kent, during the
latter stages of the Battle of Britain.

Above left: A Dewoitine D.520 fighter of GC I/III, flown by
Sous-Lieutenant Pierre Le Gloan.
Above right: Wreckage of a Fiat CR.42 fighter, shot down by RAF Gladiators in the desert.

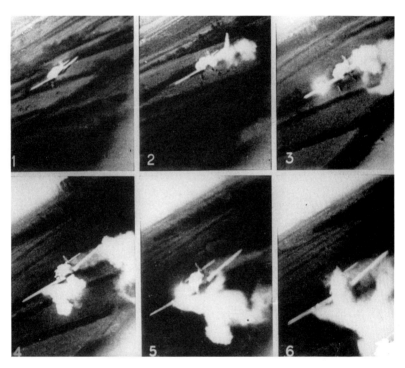

A Messerschmitt 109 falls victim to a Spitfire during the Battle of Britain.

Curtiss P-40 Tomahawk of No 112 Squadron RAF, taxiing in a cloud of desert sand.

An armourer working on a Spitfire MkV in Italy.

Above left: The Focke-Wulf Fw 190, one of the war's finest fighters, presented a powerful challenge to Allied air supremacy.
Above right: The North American P-51 Mustang was the fighter that took the war to Germany. It had enough range to escort bombers to Berlin and beyond.

The Hawker Tempest Mk.V, the most powerful piston-engined fighter of World War Two.

Tempest pilots in Normandy, July 1944.

Above left: The Messerschmitt Me 262 jet fighter, the aircraft in which the world's first jet aces scored their victories.

Above right: Final fling: on New Year's Day, 1945, large formations of German fighter-bombers attacked Allied airfields in the Low Countries. Here, two Focke-Wulfs strafe Evere, near Brussels. Luftwaffe losses in the attack were high.

No escape! A fleeing Focke-Wulf 190 falls to the guns of a
Mustang over Germany, early 1945.

Operating high-performance fighters from aircraft carriers had its problems. Here, a Sea Hurricane comes to grief in a slippery deck.

Burma, 1944. A Japanese bomber being strafed by RAF fighters. Note the Japanese personnel scattering for cover.

The Lockheed P-38 Lightning, the long-range fighter in which most USAAF aces of the Pacific War scored their victories.

This night-fighter version of the Lightning was used successfully against the Japanese in the Pacific Theatre.

a wheels-up landing. On 23 August 1942, shortly before leaving the 49 FG, Morehead shot down two Zeros, and later destroyed a Messerschmitt 109 while flying with the 1st Fighter Group in Italy. He remained in the USAF after the war, retiring with the rank of colonel.

Another pilot who had fought in the Java battle – where he destroyed four enemy bombers – was Captain Andrew Jackson Reynolds, who got out on one of the last B-17s to leave the island before the collapse. He gained another five victories during his tour with the 49th FG in Australia, and like Morehead remained in the USAF after the war to retire with the rank of colonel. Captain William J. Hennon also fought in Java, destroying three Ki 21 Sally bombers, and he added two Zeros to his score over Darwin. His sixth victory was gained on 25 April, when he chased a Zero out to sea and opened fire from a range of 100 feet. The Zero exploded and Hennon's P-40 was peppered by fragments of blazing wreckage, fortunately without sustaining serious damage.

Following the Japanese landings on New Guinea, the RAAF sent No 75 Squadron, which was also equipped with P-40E fighters, to Port Moresby to defend that vital outpost from enemy air attack. No 75 Squadron bore the brunt of the Japanese assaults until 28 April 1942, when, weary and sadly depleted, it was pulled out of the fighting and replaced by the 8th Fighter Group of the USAAF (the Army Air Corps had now been renamed Army Air Force). The 8th FG was equipped with Bell P-39 Airacobra fighters, which were hopelessly outclassed by the Zero. By October, the 49th Fighter Group had been moved to New Guinea, where its P-40s were used for both ground attack and air defence.

One pilot who went into action over New Guinea, with the 49th Group's 7th Squadron, was Captain Robert M. DeHaven, who was to score fourteen victories, most of them in the P-40, while flying with the Group. DeHaven joined the 49th Group in May 1943 and flew 25 combat missions before destroying his first enemy aircraft, a Val dive-bomber. His fifth kill was made on 25 December 1943, when he was flying a routine fighter sweep to Hansa Bay. Ground control came on the air to say that the 7th Squadron's base was under attack, and the P-40 leader – to whom DeHaven was flying as number two – adopted a new heading that would enable the Warhawks to intercept the enemy as they returned to their airfield at Madang.

The enemy fighters turned out to be a mixture of Nakajima Ki 43 Oscars and Kawasaki Ki 61 Tonys, about twenty in all. As the P-40 leader and DeHaven were lining up on a pair of Oscars, DeHaven suddenly spotted two Tonys curving round to intercept them and called out a warning. Breaking hard towards the leading Japanese fighter, DeHaven got off a high-deflection shot and then immediately turned to face the second Tony. He lost sight of his first target, but his leader saw it pitch up and the pilot bale out.

DeHaven was about to engage the second enemy fighter when his own aircraft shook to the impact of bullets. Looking in his rear-view mirror, the American saw yet another Tony, sitting a few yards behind him. He threw his P-40 into a steep dive, followed by a series of violent evasive manoeuvres. The Japanese pilot was exceptionally good and clung doggedly to the P-40, still firing and hitting his target time after time.

Suddenly, at 2,500 feet, the Japanese fighter broke away. A moment later, four more Tonys flashed overhead, going in the opposite direction. With one of those strange turns of luck that often characterise air combat, DeHaven's adversary had clearly mistaken his colleagues for P-40s. The American managed to struggle home in his battered aircraft and make a successful belly landing. There were 187 bullet holes in his P-40, the control surfaces were torn to shreds, the radio was shot to pieces and there were several leaks in the aircraft's main fuel tank. It had been the hardest battle DeHaven would ever have to fight.

Although all the pilots mentioned so far achieved the magic figure of five enemy aircraft destroyed to become aces while flying Warhawks, there were others who came very close to it. One of them was Lieutenant James P. Hagerstrom, who was one of 34 P-40 pilots of the 49th FG who engaged some 65 enemy fighters over Wewak on 23 January 1944. In the battle that followed, Hagerstrom destroyed four Zeros and a Tony, while his wingman, Lieutenant John Bodak, claimed two Zeros. Between them, the two pilots also claimed three probables. The astonishing thing about this fight was that both Americans returned to base without a single bullet hole in their aircraft. During the Korean War, flying F-86 Sabres, Hagerstrom finally reached the ranks of the aces, destroying eight MiG-15s.

There was one 49th FG pilot who became an ace twice over, scoring ten kills while flying P-40s. He achieved this in nine months of combat operations, and six of his victories were gained on just two missions. He was Captain Ernest A. Harris, commanding the 8th Squadron.

Harris opened his scoreboard on 7 January 1943, during the defence of northern Australia, when he shot down three Zeros over Markham Bay in ten minutes. On 3 March 1943 he shot down a third Zero over Lae. On 11 April he scored another triple victory, destroying two Zeros and a Val dive-bomber over Oro Bay, and on 14 May he shot down two Betty bombers, again over Oro Bay. His last victory with the 49th came on 21 September 1943, when he destroyed a Zero over the Huon Peninsula.

Like so many others, Harris chose to remain in the USAF after the war's end. He was killed in 1949, when the Republic F-84 Thunderjet he was flying was involved in a mid-air collision with another aircraft.

By the spring of 1944, the 49th Fighter Group had re-equipped in the main with the twin-engined Lockheed P-38 Lightning. The 7th Squadron continued to use P-40s for the rest of the year, and scored successes during the battle to recapture the Philippines, but it was the long-range Lightning that was to be the mainstay of the USAAF's effort in the Pacific from now on. The day of the P-40 was over; but it was the Warhawk which, often at terrible cost, had held the line in the dark days when Japan seemed invincible.

CHAPTER EIGHT

Aces over the Desert

It was 18 April 1943, and the desert war in North Africa was approaching its finale. Ten days earlier, the US II Corps, approaching from Algeria, had joined forces with General Montgomery's battle-weary Eighth Army to begin the drive northwards into Tunisia, the last stronghold of Erwin Rommel's Panzer Army Africa. At the same time, the Allied air forces had begun an all-out campaign to destroy the remnants of the *Luftwaffe* in Africa; they had also launched a series of heavy attacks on airfields in Sicily and southern Italy, where the enemy was assembling fleets to transport aircraft – Junkers 52s and massive, six-engined Messerschmitt Me 323 'Giants' – in a desperate attempt to get supplies and reinforcements through to Rommel's forces.

On this Palm Sunday, long lines of battle-ready German troops, fresh from training camps in Italy, filed aboard 90 three-engined Ju 52 transports in Sicily. There were 1,800 soldiers in all, twenty to each aircraft. At 16.30 the armada took off and set course south-westwards, flying in three immaculate Vs and keeping low over the sea to avoid detection by radar stations on Malta. With the transports came the fighter escort, 30 Me 109s and Me 110s and a few Italian Macchi C.202s.

Three hundred miles away, on the other side of the Mediterranean, the air also thundered with the roar of engines as 48 P-40 Warhawks of the USAAF's 57th and 324th Fighter Groups took off from El Djem airfield and climbed northwards over the Tunisian coast. The pilots' orders were to patrol the Cape Bon area and the Gulf of Tunis. Over Sousse, halfway to the Gulf, twelve sleek aircraft came up from the east and slipped into position above the American formation, at 15,000 feet. They were the Spitfires of No 92 Squadron, RAF.

The big fighter formation reached Cape Bon and began its patrol. For ninety minutes the pilots flew back and forth over the sea, patrolling at between 7,000 and 15,000 feet.

In the cockpit of one of the 57th Fighter Group P-40s, Captain Roy Whittaker scanned the western sky through the glare of the sinking sun. Like most of the other pilots, he was tired and bored: they had already flown one patrol that day without sighting an enemy aircraft, and now, with only minutes to go before they were due to return to base, it seemed as though they were going to be out of luck yet again.

Suddenly, something caught Whittaker's eye: the flash of sunlight on a wing, low over the sea. A moment later, he made out a large formation of enemy fighters, weaving from side to side over the water. Behind them, like a massive flight of geese, Junkers 52 transports stretched as far as the eye could see. They were flying in perfect formation as though at an air show, heading towards the Tunisian coast. It was a fighter pilot's dream.

While twelve P-40s and the Spitfires of No 92 Squadron engaged the enemy fighter escort, the remaining 36 P-40s attacked the Junkers transports. Roy Whittaker turned in behind the leading formation and fired at a pair of Ju 52s, seeing pieces fly off one of them, then he climbed away and circled for another attack. This time he was more successful; two Junkers went down in flames and a few moments later they were joined by a third. Pulling up sharply, Whittaker found the underside of an Me 109 filling his sights. He fired, and the enemy fighter spun into the sea. The American glanced at his watch; he had destroyed four enemy aircraft in three minutes.

Everywhere it was the same story. Young pilots for whom this was the first taste of combat suddenly found themselves turned into aces in a matter of minutes as one transport after another went down before their guns. Lieutenants Arthur B. Cleaveland and Richard E. Duffy destroyed five Ju 52s apiece, while another

57th Group pilot, Lieutenant MacArthur Powers, shot down four Ju 52s and an Me 109. Many other P-40 pilots scored multiple victories.

Deprived of their fighter cover, by this time scattered all over the sky by the Spitfires and Warhawks, the slow transports had no chance. Many of the Junkers pilots who escaped the initial onslaught pushed down the noses of their aircraft and headed for the coast at full throttle, intent on making a forced landing on the beach, only to be caught by the much faster fighters and sent blazing into the surf. The fighter pilots later reported how the Germans jettisoned their hatches and doors, and how German troops blazed away from the interior with rifles and light machine-guns.

In just ten minutes, for the loss of six of their own number, the allied fighters had destroyed 77 enemy aircraft – more than RAF Fighter Command had shot down during the worst day's fighting of the Battle of Britain. Fifty-nine of those aircraft were transports, and with them a thousand picked men of the Afrika Corps went to their deaths. So ended the great air battle that would go down in history as the Palm Sunday Massacre.

Four days later the Germans tried again, this time with huge Messerschmitt 323s. Sixteen aircraft, all from *Transportgeschwader* No 5 (TG 5) and fully laden with desperately-needed supplies of fuel, were heading for Tunis with a small fighter escort when they were caught off Cape Bon by two squadrons of RAF Spitfires and four squadrons of South African Air Force P-40s. In five minutes, the fighters shot down fourteen of the mighty transports and seven of their escorting fighters, leaving the coastal waters aflame with burning petrol. Two hundred and forty tons of fuel never reached the Afrika Corps that day, and of the 140 aircrew of TG 5 who took part in the operation, only nineteen survived.

It was a far cry from the days of nearly three years earlier, when – following Mussolini's declaration of war on Britain in June 1940 – Italian forces marched on Egypt, confident of an early victory and the seizure of the vital Suez Canal. At that time, the air defence of Egypt rested on three squadrons of RAF Gloster Gladiator biplane fighters. On paper, the RAF was confronted by superior numbers of Italian fighters, but many of these were obsolete and only two squadrons were equipped with Fiat CR.42s, which were roughly the equivalent of the Gladiators in terms of performance. It was between these two types of aircraft that the early desert air battles were fought.

The first air combat of the desert war took place on 14 June 1940, when seven Gladiators of No 33 Squadron, led by the CO, Squadron Leader D.V. Johnson, came upon a Caproni Ca 310 reconnaissance aircraft escorted by three Fiat CR.32s over Fort Capuzzo. Pilot Officer V.C. Woodward and Sergeant Craig destroyed the Caproni, while Flying Officer E.H. Dean shot down one of the CR.32s.

For Vernon Crompton Woodward, a Canadian from Victoria, British Columbia, it was the first of a long list of victories. Two weeks later, he destroyed two Fiat CR.32s in a dogfight over Bardia, and on 24 July he shot down a Fiat CR.42 and probably destroyed another. On the following day, while patrolling with Sergeant Slater, the two Gladiators were attacked by a dozen CR.42s which came down on them out of the sun. The Italians were apparently over-eager, and missed with their first attack. Woodward and Slater got above them and in a short space of time destroyed three CR.42s, claiming one each and sharing the third. Then Slater was shot down, and for the next few minutes Woodward was left alone to fend off a series of determined assaults, turning again and again to meet his attackers head-on. Suddenly, the Italians flew away, probably short of fuel. The exhausted Canadian flew back to base and landed safely. Climbing from the cockpit, he walked round the Gladiator to inspect the damage. Amazingly, there were only three bullet holes in the aircraft.

Woodward destroyed his next victim early in December 1940, and then, in a three-week period from 9 to 20 December, he shot down five CR.42s, probably destroyed a fifth, and damaged four more. By this time No 33 Squadron had begun to re-equip with Hurricanes, and with these aircraft it moved to Greece early in 1941 to fly bomber escort missions over Albania in support of the Greek Army, locked in bitter fighting with invading Italian forces.

At this time, No 33 Squadron was commanded by Squadron Leader Marmaduke St John Pattle, who had already established a considerable reputation as an air fighter in the Western Desert. His first taste of action came on 24 July 1940, when six Gladiators led by himself encountered eighteen Italian fighters and bombers over Sollum. Pattle destroyed one and the other Gladiator pilots accounted for three more without loss to themselves. The next day, Pattle and three other Gladiators intercepted seven enemy aircraft over Bardia and destroyed five of them, Pattle himself shooting down three.

On 4 August Pattle, now flying with No 80 Squadron, was shot down while escorting some Lysanders on a reconnaissance mission, but not before he he had disposed of two enemy aircraft. After walking through the desert for 24 hours he was picked up by a British patrol and returned to his base at Sidi Barrani. Four days later, he had his revenge. On 8 August, thirteen Gladiators – including Pattle – were carrying out an offensive patrol when 27 Fiat CR.42 biplanes were sighted near El Gobi. The Gladiators had all the advantages, attacking out of the sun, and in the dogfight that followed nine Italian aircraft were destroyed for certain, two of them by Pattle. One Gladiator pilot was killed and a second baled out safely.

In November 1940 No 80 Squadron moved to Greece, and Pattle's score began to increase rapidly. That month he destroyed two Fiat CR.42s, shared two more with other pilots and damaged two SM.79 bombers. On 2 December he shot down two Ro.37 observation biplanes, and two days later he destroyed three CR.42s, also claiming two more enemy bombers, and the next day he added another CR.42 to his list. His growing reputation as a superlative air fighter – a brilliant tactician who launched his attacks with split-second timing and who rarely missed – had an electrifying effect on the morale of the other pilots. By the end of December the Squadron had destroyed no fewer that 40 Italian aircraft for the loss in action of only six Gladiators, and the rumour that No 80 would shortly re-equip with Hawker Hurricanes brought a promise of even greater achievements to come.

The first Hurricanes arrived in Greece on 7 February, and were allocated to No 80 Squadron. Pattle's first combat in a Hurricane came on 20 February, when he shot down a Fiat G.50 fighter; the other pilots of his flight destroyed three more. In the last week of February the Greek Army launched a major offensive that was designed to push the Italians out of Albania, and during this campaign the three RAF fighter squadrons supporting the Greeks – Nos 33, 80 and 112 – scored their biggest success so far. In 90 minutes of air fighting on 27 February, while providing top cover for the Greek drive on Tepelini, the RAF pilots destroyed 27 enemy aircraft over the front line, every one of them a confirmed victory. Pattle himself shot down three Fiat CR.42s in less than three minutes.

The next day he destroyed two Fiat BR.20 bombers, and in a big air battle on 4 March he shot down two CR.42s and a G.50. Towards the end of the month he was posted to command No 33 Squadron, and he had been in his new appointment for less than a week when events took a dramatic turn for the worse. On 6 April 1941, German forces invaded both Greece and Yugoslavia, and from then on the RAF pilots began to encounter much more formidable opposition. Against the 1,200 combat aircraft of the German *Luftflotte* 4 the Allies could muster only about 200 machines, and of these only about 50 were modern Hurricanes.

Despite their numerical inferiority, the RAF fighter pilots continued to give an excellent account of themselves. On the first day of the German invasion Pattle shot down two Me 109s; the next day he shot down a CR.42; on the 9th he destroyed his first German bomber, a Junkers 88; on the 10th an Me 109 and an Me 110; on the 11th a Heinkel 111 and a Junkers 88; and on the 12th a Dornier 17 and an SM.79.

The enemy advance continued relentlessly, and by the middle of April the Greeks and the Commonwealth forces supporting them were fighting a desperate withdrawal action, all the while under heavy air attack by the *Luftwaffe*. Within a few days there were only fifteen serviceable Hurricanes left in the whole of Greece, and these were assembled at Elevsis, near Athens, under Pattle's command.

Pattle himself was now suffering from severe exhaustion, aggravated by influenza. Nevertheless he continueed to fly and fight, and on 19 April he shot down two Me 109s and a Ju 88 and shared in the destruction of a Henschel 126 observation aircraft. The next day, still feeling ill, he took off at the head of the surviving Hurricanes to intercept a formation of Junkers 88 dive-bombers which was heading for Athens, escorted by a swarm of Me 109s and 110s. Pattle led his pilots into the middle of the enemy formation, setting a 110 on fire with his first burst. A second 110 went down in flames a few moments later, and as he climbed away Pattle found himself pursued by a pair of 109s. He broke hard towards the attackers and shot down one of them;

no-one knows for certain what happened after that, only that his Hurricane tumbled like a falling leaf into the waters of Elevsis Bay, and that the pilot did not bale out.

In the confusion of the withdrawal from Greece, the subsequent desperate struggle for Crete and the Western Desert, Pattle's exploits were forgotten, except by the pilots who had served alongside him. Many of them swear that his final score was over 40 enemy aircraft destroyed, which would make him the top-scoring RAF fighter ace ahead of the generally accepted leading scorer, Group Captain J.E. Johnson. The controversy is never likely to be resolved.

One of the pilots who got out of Greece before the final collapse was Vernon Woodward, who destroyed an Me 110, damaged three more and probably destroyed a Junkers 88 in the air fight over Elevsis in which Pattle was killed. Woodward shot down eight enemy aircraft during the Greek campaign, bringing his total score at this time to nineteen. He was wounded in the leg by cannon-shell splinters during the battle for Crete. Later, while flying Hurricanes with No 274 Squadron in Libya, he destroyed a Fiat G.50, and on 12 July 1941 he shot down a Junkers 88, his last victory. He was then the top-scoring Canadian fighter pilot, but this honour eventually passed to Flight Lieutenant George Buerling, famous for his achievements in the defence of Malta, who gained 31 victories.

Although there were several Hurricane squadrons in North Africa by the end of 1941, it was the units equipped with the American-built Curtiss P-40 Tomahawk that bore the brunt of the fighting. The P-40 was generally inferior to the Messerschmitt Me 109F, its principal opponent in the desert air war, but it packed a heavy punch with its six .5-inch machine-guns, and a number of pilots achieved considerable success while flying it. One of them was an Australian, Clive Caldwell, who joined No 250 Squadron in Palestine in January 1941 and moved with it up to the Western Desert a few months later. Caldwell shot down his first enemy aircraft, an Me 109, on 26 June, and the last day of the month he destroyed two Ju 87 Stukas, as well as sharing in the destruction of an Me 110. On 7 July, he added a Fiat G.50 to his score during an offensive sweep over Bardia.

On 29 August, he was 'bounced' by a pair of Me 109s while on a defensive patrol over Tobruk, and despite being wounded in the shoulder, back and leg by shell splinters he turned the tables on the enemy and shot one of them down into the sea. He claimed another Me 109 on 23 November; and then, on 5 December, came his most successful day so far. That morning, Caldwell was leading nineteen Tomahawks of Nos 250 and 112 Squadrons on an offensive sweep west of El Gobi when they encountered some 60 Stukas, escorted by Me 109s. In a running battle lasting half an hour, the Tomahawk pilots shot down no fewer than 27 of the slow dive-bombers, Caldwell himself claiming five. It was the most disastrous loss suffered by the *Luftwaffe* in the Western Desert Campaign, and would be surpassed only by the massacre that took place on Palm Sunday, 1943.

In January 1942 Caldwell was promoted to squadron leader and given command of No 112 Squadron, whose Tomahawks carried a distinctive shark's mouth marking on their noses. A few weeks later the squadron re-equipped with P-40E Kittyhawks, with which it carried out both ground attack and fighter missions. Caldwell continued to lead No 112 until May 1942, by which time he had scored twenty victories; he subsequently returned to Australia to command a newly-formed Spitfire wing at Darwin, and as we shall see in a later chapter he would add to his score in operations against the Japanese.

The officer who replaced Caldwell as CO of No 112 Squadron was a Londoner, Squadron Leader Billy Drake, who had been commissioned into the RAF in 1937. In 1939–40 he served in France with No 1 Squadron, flying Hurricanes, and shot down three Me 109s before being shot down and wounded himself. He was evacuated to England and, after several months in hospital, served with No 91 Squadron, No 53 Operational Training Unit and No 128 Squadron, the latter flying Hurricanes in West Africa, before taking command of No 112 Squadron in May 1942.

Drake scored his first desert kills in June 1942, during the fierce air fighting over the Gazala Line; he destroyed two Me 109s and probably destroyed another. After a rest from operations in August, No 112 Squadron came back into the line on 1 September, and Drake celebrated his return by destroying two Stukas near Quat-el-Abd. During the following weeks he shot down an Me 109 and shared in the destruction of several more enemy aircraft.

His most hectic week was in October, when No 112 Squadron flew intensively in support of the Eighth Army's offensive at El Alamein. On 26 October, Drake shot down an Me 109; the next day he destroyed a Macchi 202; and on the last day of the month he claimed a Stuka. On 5 November he destroyed an Me 109 and damaged another; on the 15th he shot down a Heinkel 111, and four days later he destroyed an Me 110 and damaged its companion. On 11 December, while on a bomber escort mission, he shot down a Macchi 202 after a long chase up the coast, but then his Kittyhawk was jumped by half a dozen Me 109s and was so badly hit that Drake had to make a forced landing, fortunately in friendly territory. Two days later, he shared in the destruction of an Me 109 with another pilot; it was his last combat in North Africa, and a few weeks later he relinquished command of No 112 Squadron. He later commanded a Spitfire wing in Italy, where he increased his score to 24 enemy aircraft destroyed. He survived the war, and was granted a permanent RAF commission in 1948.

One of the leading RAF fighter pilots in the Western Desert also flew with No 112 Squadron. He was Neville Duke, who was to achieve even greater fame in the post-war years as Chief Test Pilot with Hawker Aircraft Ltd, his name synonymous with the Hunter jet fighter in which he briefly captured the World Air Speed Record.

When Duke joined No 112 Squadron in November 1941 he already had two enemy aircraft to his credit, destroyed over northern France while flying Spitfires with No 92 Squadron. Within days of his arrival in the desert he shot down an Me 109 and shared a Fiat CR.42; he was then shot down himself in a fight near El Gobi, but was picked up by friendly troops and returned to his base. He was shot a second time on 5 December, having just added a Macchi 202 to his score, and this time was wounded in the leg, which put him out of action for a fortnight. On his first sortie after returning to the squadron, he destroyed an Me 109 and probably destroyed two Stukas.

By March 1942, Duke had eight enemy aircraft to his credit. His tour with No 112 Squadron was now over and he was posted to a fighter school in Egypt as an instructor. When he returned to action in November 1942 it was with his original unit, No 92 Squadron, which had moved to the Middle East and was stationed at Sidi Barrani. The squadron now began a series of leapfrogging movements, flying from one forward airstrip to another in the wake on the Eighth Army's advance, and in January 1943 Duke shot down three Macchi 202s and a pair of Junkers 87s.

He was now promoted to flight lieutenant and awarded a Bar to his DFC, which he had earned in the previous year.

On 1 March 1943, while he was acting CO of No 92 Squadron, Duke shot down two Macchi 202s in one sortie, and in that same week he destroyed five more enemy aircraft, all Me 109s. He shot down another Me 109 on 29 March, followed by two SM.79 bombers on 16 April, shortly before his second tour of operations in North Africa came to an end.

After another spell as an instructor, he was given command of No 145 Squadron, flying Spitfires in Italy. During the Italian campaign he destroyed six more enemy aircraft, making him the top-scoring pilot of Middle East Command with 28 confirmed kills.

One of No 145 Squadron's previous commanding officers was Lance Wade, an American from Tucson, Texas who had volunteered to fly and fight with the Royal Air Force during the dark days of 1940, long before the United States entered the war. Wade arrived in the Middle East in September 1941 and flew Hurricanes with No 33 Squadron, destroying three enemy aircraft and damaging several more during his first operational tour. He was shot down once, 25 miles inside enemy territory, and walked through the desert to the British lines.

After a short rest from operations, he returned to No 33 Squadron and scored a double success on 28 May 1942, shooting down a Ju 87 and a Macchi 202. On 9 June he shot down an Me 109 over Bir Hakeim, and in July he destroyed two more Me 109s and a Ju 88. Further successes raised his total of confirmed victories to fifteen by the middle of October, when he was promoted to squadron leader and given command of No 145 Squadron. Wade destroyed eight more enemy aircraft over North Africa; he was then promoted to wing commander and given command of a Spitfire wing in Italy, where he shot down a further two enemy aircraft to bring his final score to 25.

In January, 1944, Lance Wade was flying an Auster light aircraft on a liaison visit to an airfield in Italy. For a reason that was never discovered, it went into a spin at low altitude and crashed, exploding on impact. Wade was killed instantly.

During the latter months of its operations in North Africa, No 145 Squadron had a rather extraordinary unit attached to it. It was commanded by a Pole, Squadron Leader Stanislaw Skalski. A regular officer in the Polish Air Force before the war, Skalski destroyed 6¼ enemy aircraft during the Polish campaign, flying PZL P.11 fighters with No 142 Squadron. He reached England in January 1940 and fought his way through the Battle of Britain with No 501 Squadron, destroying four enemy aircraft and damaging two more before being shot down and wounded on 6 September. He claimed two Focke-Wulf 190s and damaged an Me 109 in the spring of 1942 and then commanded No 317 'Wilenski' Squadron, a Polish Spitfire unit.

He arrived in North Africa early in 1943, leading a unit of experienced fighter pilots known as the Polish Fighting Team – or, more popularly, as 'Skalski's Circus'. Flying Spitfire Mk 9s – the first unit to operate this make of the Spitfire in North Africa – the Poles were attached to No 145 Squadron, and in eight weeks of operations their exploits became legendary. During that two-month period, they shot down more enemy aircraft than any other Polish fighter unit in 1943, and the pilots achieved such reputations that they were subsequently offered posts as commanding officers of other RAF fighter squadrons.

Skalski, who shot down two Me 109s and a Ju 88 over Tunisia, became the first Pole to command an RAF fighter squadron, the famous No 601 (County of London) Squadron of the Auxiliary Air Force. Later, in 1944, he was promoted to wing commander and led No 2 (Polish) Wing for the rest of the war, flying Mustangs. He ended the war with a score of nineteen enemy aircraft destroyed, including those he had claimed over Poland in September 1939.

In 1946 he returned to Poland – not to a hero's welcome, but to be imprisoned for a time by the Russians, like so many of his countrymen who had fought alongside the British and Americans. On his release, he drove a taxi in Warsaw. For the Poles, in these post-war years, the freedom for which they had striven for so long was a distant ideal.

On the enemy side of the fence, a great deal of attention has been paid to the activities of the *Luftwaffe* in North Africa, to the detriment of the achievements of Italian airmen. The fact is, that many of the Italian fighter pilots encountered by the RAF and commonwealth air forces in the Middle East were skilled and highly experienced, having fought in the Spanish Civil War; they would often stay and fight, sometimes against overwhelming odds, in situations where German pilots would readily break off combat.

One of the top-scoring Italian fighter pilots in Spain was Captain Mario Visentini, who destroyed twelve Republican aircraft. In 1940 he flew Fiat CR.42s in East Africa and claimed five British aircraft destroyed – including three Gloster Gladiators – but on 11 February 1941, with British forces on the offensive, he was killed in a gallant attempt to take off from his airfield with two ground crew members strapped to the wings of his fighter.

The top-scoring Italian fighter pilot to survive the war was Captain Franco Bordoni-Bisleri. In October 1940 he went to Belgium with the Italian Expeditionary Air Corps, which was intended to be Italy's contribution to the air offensive against Britain but which did not arrive until the main battle was over and which suffered heavy losses against the RAF's Spitfires and Hurricanes in the few operations it carried out. Bordoni-Bisleri then went to North Africa with the 18th Group in 1941, claiming five victories while flying a CR.42. During a second North African tour in 1942, this time flying Macchi 202s, he claimed seven more enemy aircraft destroyed. In 1943, during the defence of the Rome area, he raised his score to nineteen; his last victory came on 5 September, only days before the Italians signed a separate armistice with the Allies.

The first claim made against the RAF in the desert war fell to Captain Franco Lucchini, who had destroyed five enemy aircraft in Spain. On 14 June 1940, while flying a CR.42 of the 4th Wing from Tobruk, he shot down a Gladiator, the first of his 21 kills in World War Two. In addition to his own score, Lucchini shared in 51 other victories in the course of 244 operational sorties flown over North Africa and Italy. His last victim was an RAF Spitfire, which he destroyed over Sicily on 5 July 1943. Minutes later, he was shot down and killed by the rear gunner of a B-17, one of the bombers the Spitfire had been escorting.

Lucchini shared joint first place in the list of Italian aces with Major Adriano Visconti, who also had 26 victories, including five in Spain. Visconti, who led the 1st Fighter Group, gained most of his victories in the defence of Sicily and Italy, shooting down fourteen Allied aircraft. After the armistice he fought on the German side with the air force of the Italian Socialist Republic in northern Italy, gaining seven more victories. He was murdered by Italian Communist partisans in Milan on 29 April 1945.

Of the other leading Italian aces, First Sergeant Teresio Martinoli (22 victories) was killed in a flying accident at Naples in July 1944; Second Lieutenant Leonardo Ferrulli (20 victories) was shot down and killed over Sicily on 5 July 1943 in a lone dogfight with 30 Allied fighters, having destroyed two of his opponents; and Sergeant Luigi Gorrini (19 victories) destroyed eight enemy aircraft in twenty days in August 1943, six of them four-engined American bombers. He was wounded on the last day of the month, but later fought alongside the Germans and added four more kills to his score. Gorrini, unlike many of his colleagues, survived the war.

But in North Africa it was the *Luftwaffe*'s fighter pilots who received the accolades and the publicity, and one particular pilot undoubtedly led the field. He was Lieutenant Hans-Jochen Marseille, who arrived in North Africa in April 1941 with No 3 Squadron, Fighter Wing 27 (III/JG 27). Marseille did not have a good reputation; phrases such as 'showed bravado and played pranks while under training' and 'committed offences in contravention of flying regulations' appeared over and over again in his personal file. He seemed to be dogged by bad luck, too; he had scored eight victories while flying over the Channel area in the autumn of 1940, but at the same time he had been forced to bale out of no fewer than six Messerschmitts, as a consequence of battle damage or engine failure. It was by no means good arithmetic.

Shortly after his arrival in the desert, Marseille's aircraft suffered an engine failure and he had to make a forced landing 500 miles from base. Hitching a ride on an Italian supply truck, Marseille reached a depot where he managed to convince a German general that he was a squadron commander. The general placed his staff car at the young airman's disposal and sent him on his way with the following valedictory message: 'You can repay me with 50 victories.' Marseille promised to do this, never dreaming that the promise would be fulfilled three times over.

In April 1942, by which time his score had risen to 48 enemy aircraft destroyed, Marseille was given command of III/JG 27. He was much less headstrong now, having been given a sharp warning by JG 27's commander, Major Eduard Neumann, and had devoted much of his time to improving his air fighting tactics and marksmanship. As his high score showed, the hard work was paying dividends.

On 3 June 1942, during the battle for the Gazala Line, Marseille led III/JG 27 on a mission to Bir Hakeim, escorting Stukas which were dive-bombing the Free French positions there. The Stukas were attacked by the Tomahawks of No 5 Squadron, South African Air Force, which had inflicted heavy losses on the dive-bombers during earlier raids.

Together with his wingman, Sergeant Reiner Pöttgen, Marseille dived his Me 109 into the middle of the South Africans, who, believing that they were being attacked by a far superior force, immediately formed a defensive circle. Marseille got inside it, turning steeply, and gave a P-40 a short burst. The fighter went down vertically and exploded in the desert. Marseille's tactics were unorthodox; turning continually inside the circle of enemy fighters, keeping his airspeed low, he fired in short, accurate bursts. In less than twelve minutes, he had accounted for five more Tomahawks, all of which were seen to crash by Pöttgen.

During the next few days Marseille destroyed fourteen more aircraft. His score was now 91 and, as he approached the magic figure of 100, the other pilots of JG 27 were laying bets on when he would claim his 100th victory. On 16 June he shot down four aircraft, and the following day he claimed a further six, making his score 101. After that, he was sent home on leave. He was away for two months, and when he returned he found that considerable changes had taken place.

A fierce argument had broken out between Rommel and Field Marshal Kesselring, the commander of the German forces in the Mediterranean theatre. In June, when Tobruk fell to the Germans, Rommel had declared his intention to push straight on to the Nile Delta and Cairo, giving the British no time to regroup their forces. Kesselring's argument was that such a move would create an enormous logistics problem for the *Luftwaffe*, whose crews were exhausted and aircraft badly in need of overhaul. Moreover, the strength of the British Desert Air Force was continuing to grow and the *Luftwaffe* was in no position to mount attacks on its airfields; this meant that if Rommel persisted in an all-out drive on Cairo, there was no guarantee that the *Luftwaffe* would be able to provide the necessary air support. Rommel, however, emerged victorious from the contest of wills and the advance continued. The *Luftwaffe* threw its dwindling resources into the battle, attacking enemy supply depots and troop concentrations. At the end of June, JG 27 took its Me 109s to Sidi Barrani, and for days on end the pilots flew sortie after sortie. Rommel's drive finally ground to a halt before El Alamein, and it was at this point that Marseille returned to the battle.

For a week he saw little action. Then, on 1 September, Rommel made a last attempt to break through the Eighth Army's defences, and fierce air battles developed over the front when the *Luftwaffe* put every available fighter into the air in a maximum effort. For Marseille, the day began at 08.28 when he shot down a Kittyhawk. A second P-40 followed quickly, and ten minutes later he claimed a pair of Spitfires. In an incredible ten-minute period between 10.55 and 11.05, while escorting Stukas on a raid against Alem el Halfa, he claimed no fewer than eight Kittyhawks. In a third sortie between 17.47 and 17.53 he destroyed five more aircraft south of Imayid, raising his score for the day to the unbelievable total of seventeen.

Later, this claim was to be the subject of controversy. It was bitterly contested by the RAF, who stated that Marseille's claim exceeded the total British losses for that day. Yet every one of Marseille's claims on 1 September was confirmed by his wingmen, who had noted times and locations. Moreover, the losses of the RAF, Australian and South African fighter squadrons for 1 September, taken together, did in fact exceed the claims of all German fighter pilots by about ten per cent. Two days later, Marseille was awarded the Diamonds to the Knight's Cross. He was now the *Luftwaffe*'s most highly-decorated pilot, possessing the Knight's Cross with Oak Leaves and Swords, and the Italian Gold Medal for Bravery, the latter being one of only three awarded in World War Two.

During September 1942, Marseille's score rose to 158 enemy aircraft destroyed. His 158th victim, a Spitfire, almost succeeded in shooting him down, but Marseille gained the advantage and despatched his opponent after a dogfight that lasted fifteen minutes.

It was his last victory. On 30 September, together with eight other Me 109s, he took off to provide top cover for a formation of Stukas. The dive-bombers attacked their targets without incident; no enemy aircraft were sighted and the Me 109s turned for home, their job completed. At 11.35, as the fighter formation cruised at 4,500 feet, Marseille's voice suddenly came over the radio, telling the others that there was smoke in his cockpit and that he could no longer see clearly. The other pilots saw him open the small ventilation hatch in the side of the canopy, and a stream of dense smoke poured out. Marseille kept repeating that he was unable to see, and the others passed directions to him over the radio. Ground control, which had heard his radio call, advised him to bale out, but the Messerschmitts were still three minutes' flying time away from the German lines and Marseille refused. He had a horror of being taken prisoner.

The smoke grew worse, pouring back from the cockpit and engulfing the rear fuselage and tail. At last, the formation entered friendly territory. The other pilots saw Marseille jettison his cockpit canopy, and a second later he fell from the cockpit as he turned the Messerschmitt over on its back. His body seemed to strike the tailplane a glancing blow, then dropped away towards the desert. There was no parachute.

They buried Jochen Marseille where he fell. A few weeks later, the tanks of Montgomery's Eighth Army rolled past the spot.

CHAPTER NINE

By Daylight to Germany

The Battle of Britain was over, and now, in the spring of 1941, RAF Fighter Command was going over to the offensive, with fighter wings – each of three squadrons – carrying out offensive 'sweeps' over France with the object of bringing the *Luftwaffe* to battle. This was a different kind of fighting; not the hectic, day-in, day-out warfare of the previous summer, when survival was as much a matter of luck as expertise, and young pilots – many of whom had only a few hours of experience on Hurricanes or Spitfires – were fortunate to come through their first encounters with the *Luftwaffe* in one piece; this was a scientific form of air warfare, cleverly directed by men who were already experienced fighter leaders, who were constantly evolving new tactics, and who shepherded their untried pilots until they could hold their own in action.

Men like Squadron Leader Jamie Rankin, a Scot from Porto-bello, Edinburgh, who had originally joined the Fleet Air Arm but later transferred to the RAF. When Rankin was appointed to command No 92 Squadron at RAF Biggin Hill in March 1941 it was already the top-scoring unit in Fighter Command, and its score increased steadily under Rankin's dynamic leadership. Rankin himself opened his score with No 92 by destroying a Heinkel He 59 floatplane and damaging an Me 109 on 5 April. This was followed by another confirmed 109 on the 24th, and in June – a month of hectic air fighting over France

102

– he shot down seven more 109s, together with one probable.

Rankin went to great lengths to give his wingmen – who were usually newcomers to the squadron – a chance to 'have a go' at the enemy. One pilot who flew with him was Pilot Officer Jim Rosser; he was actually a member of No 72 Squadron, which was also part of the Biggin Hill Wing, but as Rosser explains:

'We didn't always fly operationally with our own squadrons. On this occasion Jamie Rankin was leading the wing and I was flying as his number two, which was a considerable privilege. The *Luftwaffe* was up in strength and there was an almighty free-for-all, during which the wing got split up. I clung to Jamie's tail like grim death, and as we were heading for the Channel he suddenly called up over the R/T and said: "There's a Hun at two o'clock below – have a go!" I looked down ahead and to the right and there, sure enough, was a 109, flying along quite sedately a few thousand feet lower down. I dived after him, levelled out astern and opened fire. He began to smoke almost at once and fell away in a kind of sideslip. A moment later, flames streamed from him.'

A lot of young pilots got their first break that way, while flying with Rankin. And most of them felt the same as Jim Rosser: with Jamie guarding your tail, you didn't have much to worry about except shooting down the Hun in your sights. Rankin later became leader of the Biggin Hill Wing, completed three tours of operations on Spitfires and destroyed 21 enemy aircraft.

No 72 Squadron's commanding officer in the spring of 1941 was Squadron Leader Desmond Sheen, an Australian who had begun his operational career with the squadron before the war. In April 1940 he had been posted to No 212 Squadron, and during the next few months had flown photo-reconnaissance sorties all over western Europe in specially-modified Spitfires, returning to No 72 Squadron just in time to take part in the Battle of Britain. Sheen was to lead No 72 Squadron on sweeps over occupied France for eight months, from March to November 1941. By that time he had flown 260 operational hours and had destroyed six enemy aircraft, probably destroyed two, and damaged five.

Sheen surrounded himself with a first-rate fighting team, and the leadership of his subordinate commanders was to emerge in more ways than one during that spring and summer of 1941.

Jim Rosser remembers,

'Once, we were on our way back home after a sweep, heading for Manston as usual to refuel, when the weather clamped down. I knew Manston well by this time, and I just managed to scrape in, together with four or five other pilots. Many of the others, however, were relatively new boys and they were in trouble. Then one of our 72 Squadron flight commanders, Ken Campbell, came up over the radio and told everybody to get into a circle and stay put above the murk. One by one he guided them down, wingtip to wingtip, until they were safely on the ground. When he eventually landed, I don't think he had enough fuel left to taxi in. More than one pilot owed his life to Ken that day.'

In the summer of 1942, the RAF Spitfire wings based in southern England were given the task of escorting the four-engined heavy bombers of the US Eighth Air Force, which were beginning to carry out attacks on targets in France and the Low Countries as a preliminary to the planned all-out bombing offensive against Germany. On these relatively short-range operations the Spitfire escort was effective, but when it came to attacks on targets in Germany itself the story was very different, because even with drop tanks the Spitfires did not have sufficient combat radius to escort the bombers further than northern Holland. The first raid on Germany was made by 55 B-17s on 27 January 1943, and took the enemy defences completely by surprise. The Fortresses unloaded their bombs on the docks at Wilhelmshaven and were opposed by only a handful of enemy fighters; the B-17 gunners claimed to have shot down seven of the latter, while three bombers failed to return.

The Germans quickly realised that frontal attacks on the heavily-armed bombers were the best solution, and when the Americans attacked Wilhelmshaven again on 26 February 1943 they lost seven bombers. The end of them was described by Lieutenant Heinz Knocke, a Messerschmitt 109 pilot with II/JG 2, who was to end the war with a score of 52 enemy aircraft destroyed, the majority of them four-engined heavy bombers.

'I come in for a second frontal attack, this time from a little below. I keep on firing until I have to swerve to avoid a collision. My salvoes register this time. I drop away below. As I swing round I turn my head. Flames are spreading along the bottom of the fuselage of my Liberator. It sheers away from the formation in a wide sweep to the right.

'Twice more I come in to attack, this time diving from above the tail. I am met by heavy defensive fire. My plane shudders from the recoil of the two cannon and the 13-millimetre guns. I watch my cannon shell-bursts rake along the top of the fuselage and right wing, and I hang on to the stick with both hands. The fire spreads along the right wing. The inside engine stops. Suddenly the wing breaks off altogether. The body of the stricken monster plunges vertically, spinning into the depths. A long black trail of smoke marks its descent. One of the crew attempts to bale out. But his parachute is in flames. Poor devil! The body somersaults and falls to the ground like a stone.

'At an altitude of 3,000 feet there is a tremendous explosion, which causes the spinning fuselage to disintegrate. Fragments of blazing wreckage land on a farm 200 or 300 yards from the Zwischenahn airfield, and the exploding fuel tanks set the farm buildings on fire. . .'

In January 1943, the USAAF's 4th and 56th Fighter Groups in England began to receive the first examples of a new fighter, the Republic P-47 Thunderbolt, a big, radial-engined fighter with an armament of six .50 machine-guns. It was still incapable of escorting the American daylight bombers into Germany, but its range was much better than the Spitfire's and it could extend fighter cover for a considerably greater distance along the bombers' route.

The 4th Fighter Group was composed of men who had flown with the three American 'Eagle' squadrons in the RAF, and many of them had considerable combat experience. The 4th FG's first commander was Chesley G. Peterson, a colonel at the age of only 23, who had commanded No 71 Eagle Squadron in the RAF. He had six confirmed victories, and gained another before his place as commander of the 4th FG was assumed by Colonel Don Blakeslee.

Blakeslee, like many other American volunteers, had joined the RCAF, and on arriving in England in May 1941 he had been assigned to No 401 Squadron. After that he flew with No 133 Eagle Squadron; when he took over the 4th FG he had two confirmed kills, plus a number of probables and damaged. On 15 April 1943 Blakeslee became the first Thunderbolt pilot to destroy an enemy aircraft, shooting down a Focke-Wulf 190 over the French coast. Later, he was to increase his total to 15½.

The other Thunderbolt unit in England, the 56th Fighter Group, did not receive its full complement of P-47s for several weeks, and it was not until April 1943 that it was declared operational. The 56th FG was commanded by Colonel Hubert 'Hub' Zemke, a remarkably able fighter leader whose personal score was to rise to 17¾ before his combat days ended. Many of the best-known USAAF aces of the European Theatre were to cut their teeth with Zemke's 'Wolfpack', as the 56th FG became known; men like Major Robert S. Johnson, who went on to become the first American pilot to match the score of the World War One US air ace, Eddie Rickenbacker, with 26 enemy aircraft destroyed, and who was to gain two more victories on top of that; Francis Gabreski, who would become the third-ranking US air ace with a score of 28, and who would add six and a half MiG-15s to it in action over Korea; Walker Mahurin, with 21 victories in World War Two and three and a half more in Korea; and David C. Schilling, who gained 22½ victories, five of them in one action on 23 December 1944.

The Eighth Air Force's first ace, however, belonged to another Thunderbolt unit, the 78th Fighter Group. This had arrived in England late in 1942, equipped with Lockheed P-38 Lightnings, but these had been transferred to North Africa soon afterwards as replacements for the P-38 groups there, which had suffered badly in the air battles over Tunisia. The 78th FG re-equipped with Thunderbolts in February, and in May Captain Charles P. London scored his first victory. Two more fell to his guns in the weeks that followed, and then, on 30 July, he destroyed a Focke-Wulf 190 and a Messerschmitt 109 to raise his score to five.

Another Thunderbolt ace of 1943, whose name is little known, was Lieutenant Walter C. Beckham of the 353rd Fighter Group, who destroyed eight enemy aircraft in just seven missions. On 10 October 1943 – it was the middle of a very bad week for the American daylight bombers, a week in which they lost 148 aircraft and nearly 1,500 aircrew – Beckham was leading a flight of Thunderbolts escorting a badly mauled bomber formation out of enemy territory when the bombers came under attack by enemy fighters. In the ensuing battle, Beckham destroyed two Me 210s and an Me 110 before his ammunition ran out. He ended the war as a colonel, with eighteen enemy aircraft to his credit.

While the Thunderbolts shepherded the bombers out of Germany, the RAF's Spitfires came out to meet them over Holland and Belgium. The RAF fighter pilots keenly felt the Spitfire's lack of range, which prevented them from doing more to help. One pilot who led his Spitfires into action during that black week in October 1943 was Group Captain Johnnie Johnson, who later wrote:

'It was a clear afternoon, and we first saw their contrails many miles away, as well as the thinner darting contrails of the enemy fighters above and on either flank. As we closed the gap we could see that they had taken a terrible mauling, for there were gaping holes in their precise formations. Some Fortresses were gradually losing height, and a few stragglers, lagging well behind, were struggling to get home on three engines.

'We swept well behind the stragglers and drove off a few 109s and 110s, but the great air battle was over, and what a fight it must have been, because more than half the bombers we nursed across the North Sea were shot up. One or two ditched in the sea, and many others, carrying dead and badly injured crew members, had to make crash-landings. How we longed for more drop tanks, so that some of the many hundreds of Spitfires based in Britain could play their part in the great battles over Germany. . .'

In the late summer of 1943, the only fighter in operational service in the European Theatre that was capable of escorting the Fortresses and Liberators all the way to Berlin and back was the Lockheed P-38. Four fighter groups were equipped with the P-38 in England, starting with the 55th FG in September 1943, but although the Lightnings usually managed to hold their own in combat, they were generally inferior to *Luftwaffe* fighters at altitudes of over 20,000 feet, which was where most of the air battles took place. The Lightning was not the answer.

The answer was the North American P-51 Mustang. Designed in 1940 to meet an RAF requirement for a fast, heavily-armed fighter capable of operating effectively at heights of over 20,000 feet, the RAF actually used the Mustang as a high-speed ground attack and tactical reconnaissance fighter from July 1942. It did not enter service with the USAAF until 1943, and the first Mustang unit arrived in Britain in November that year. This was the 354th Fighter Group, equipped with P-51Bs powered by Packard-built Rolls-Royce Merlin engines, which made all the difference to the fighter's performance.

Based at Boxted, near Colchester, the 354th FG initially came under the command of the Ninth Air Force. On 1 December the Group's Mustangs took off on their first operational mission – a sweep over Belgium and the Pas de Calais. The 23 pilots who took part were led by Colonel Don Blakeslee of the Debden-based 4th Fighter Group, flying a Thunderbolt. On 5 December the 354th FG – now under the operational control of the Eighth Air Force – flew the first P-51 mission to Amiens, but the *Luftwaffe* failed to appear and the Mustang pilots returned to base without having fired their guns in anger.

On 13 December the 354th flew the longest fighter mission of the war up to that date when the Mustangs – together with P-38 Lightnings of the 55th Fighter Group – escorted B-17s to Kiel and back, a round trip of 1,000 miles. Three days later, the Mustangs once again penetrated deep into Germany on an escort mission to Bremen, and it was on this raid that the Group's first enemy aircraft – an Me 110 – was destroyed by Lieutenant Charles F. Gumm of the 355th Squadron. Charles Gumm went on to become the 354th Fighter Group's first ace, destroying six enemy aircraft. He was tragically killed on 1 March 1944, when he suffered engine failure during a training sortie not far from his base. While turning steeply at low altitude in an attempt to avoid the little village of Nayland, his wing struck a tree and the Mustang crashed, killing its pilot.

By the end of the year the 354th FG had shot down eight enemy aircraft for the loss of eight Mustangs. It was not an encouraging result, and the pilots entered the new year determined to increase their success. Their chance came on 5 January 1944, when they once again escorted B-17s to Kiel; the American formation was attacked by shoals of Messerschmitt 110s and Focke-Wulf 190s and a fierce battle developed. When it ended, the Mustang pilots had claimed the destruction of eighteen enemy aircraft for no loss.

The *Luftwaffe* was up in strength again on 11 January, when the 354th escorted the Fortresses to Aschersleben. The bomber formation was repeatedly attacked by enemy fighters from the moment it crossed the coast; by the time the target was reached the bomber groups had become dislocated and the escorting Mustangs scattered all over the sky.

One of the Mustang pilots on this mission was Major James H. Howard. He was already an ace and a highly experienced fighter pilot, having shot down six Japanese aircraft while flying P-40s with the American Volunteer Group in Burma. Now, high over Germany, Howard found himself alone, the only Mustang accompanying a group of Fortresses which was about to be attacked by over 30 Messerschmitt 110s.

Howard went straight for the enemy fighters in a head-on attack, destroying one Me 110 immediately. Disconcerted, the rest scattered in all directions as his Mustang sped through them. The Germans formed up for a second attempt and once again Howard broke them up, sending another fighter down in flames. It was only the beginning. Three more times the enemy attacked, and three more times Howard fought them off single-handed. During the two final attacks, only one of the Mustang's guns was working, but Howard managed to shoot down a third enemy fighter and damage at least three more. At last, probably short of fuel or ammunition, the Germans broke off the action and dived away.

For his exploit, Major Howard later received the Congressional Medal of Honor. He was the only British-based fighter pilot to win the highest US decoration for valour during the Second World War. He later increased his score to twelve. He remained in the USAF after the war, retiring with the rank of brigadier-general.

On 11 February the 354th's Mustangs again fought their way through strong *Luftwaffe* opposition to Frankfurt, claiming fourteen enemy aircraft destroyed for the loss of two of their own number. One of the latter was Colonel Kenneth R. Martin, the Group's commander. Himself an ace with five victories, Martin was forced to bale out when he collided with an Me 110; he survived the experience and spent the rest of the war in prison camp. Command of the 354th was assumed by James Howard, and during the last week of February he led the Group in its longest penetration mission so far – a 1,100-mile round trip to Leipzig. During this raid, the Mustang pilots claimed another sixteen enemy aircraft destroyed.

Meanwhile, three other USAAF fighter groups in England had become operational in the Mustang during February 1944. In the Ninth Air Force, the 354th FG was joined by the 363rd FG on 22 February, while on 11 February the first Mustang group within the Eighth Air Force, the 357th, flew its first operational mission, a fighter sweep over Rouen. The Eighth Air Force's second Mustang group was Don Blakeslee's 4th, which exchanged its P-47s for P-51s on 27 February. Less than 24 hours later, Blakeslee was leading the group into action on an escort mission over France; his pilots had less than an hour's flying time on the Mustang!

There was considerable rivalry between the Mustang and Thunderbolt fighter groups, and the fact that on more than one occasion Mustangs returned to base badly shot up after being mistaken for Messerschmitt 109s by Thunderbolt pilots served to intensify it. The rivalry was particularly keen between the 354th and Hub Zemke's 56th 'Wolfpack' Fighter Group. In the summer of 1943, Zemke's pilots had claimed the destruction of 100 German aircraft in 86 days. Early in 1944 the 354th went all out to better this score, but on 21 February – their 83rd day of operations – the tally of the Mustang pilots stood at 92 enemy aircraft destroyed. By nightfall that same day, however, the 354th's score had risen to 103, and the following day twelve more enemy aircraft were claimed during an escort mission to Aschersleben.

On 6 March 1944 Allied fighters appeared in the sky over Berlin for the first time when Don Blakeslee's 4th Fighter Group escorted B-17s to the German capital. What followed was one of the most bitterly contested air battles of the war; when it ended the Americans had lost 69 bombers and eleven fighters, but the *Luftwaffe* lost 80 aircraft – almost half the defending force. During March alone, 'Blakeslee's Bachelors' claimed 156 German aircraft confirmed, together with eight probables; of these, 100 were claimed from 18 March to 1 April inclusive.

Although these claims were undoubtedly greatly exaggerated in the whirl of combat, there were sure signs that the *Luftwaffe* was beginning to weaken. As one American pilot put it; 'The German fighters could no longer retreat to safety. The Mustangs had them with their backs against the wall.'

What was particularly serious for the *Luftwaffe* was that the great air battles over German soil were costing the lives of their most experienced fighter leaders. One of them was Lieutenant-Colonel Wolf-Dietrich Wilcke, *Kommodore* of JG 3 'Udet', which had recently been moved to Germany from the Southern sector of the eastern front; Wilcke already had 137 Russian aircraft to his credit when he arrived back in Germany, and he subsequently destroyed a further 25 American fighters and bombers to bring his score to 162. He was killed in action on 23 March 1944. JG 3 had already lost another leading ace in November 1943, not long after it was re-deployed to Germany; he was Major Kurt Brändle, who had gained 170 kills on the Eastern Front and a further ten in the west before he was shot down and killed.

Then there was Colonel Hans Philip, *Kommodore* of JG 1, who destroyed 206 enemy aircraft – 28 of them American – before his death in action in October 1943; Captain Joachim Kirschner of JG 27, whose score at the time of his death over Germany on 17 December 1943 was 188, twenty claimed in the west; Colonel Egon Mayer, *Kommodore* of JG 2 'Richthofen', all of whose 102 victories were claimed on the Western Front and who was shot down by Mustangs on 2 March 1944; and finally Walter 'Gulle' Oesau of Battle of Britain fame, shot down after claiming his 125th victory on 11 May 1944. As a tribute, JG 1 was named after him.

Others survived, among them famous names such as Adolf Galland, who continued to fly and fight even though he was theoretically bound to a desk in his post of general in charge of fighters. In the spring of 1944, Galland found out what it was like to meet the Mustang in combat. On 8 March, together with Johannes Trautloft, another fighter ace, he took off to intercept the huge force of American bombers on its way to Berlin. The two pilots came upon a straggling B-17 and Galland shot it down, Trautloft having turned for home with jammed guns. Then a flight of Mustangs pounced, and Galland found himself fleeing for his life. He extracted every last ounce of power out of his Focke-Wulf 190, but he was unable to shake off his pursuers and bullets streamed past his aircraft, unpleasantly close. In desperation, he employed an old trick that had saved his life once before, during the Battle of Britain; he fired off everything he had into the open air ahead

111

of him. Grey smoke trails from his guns streamed back towards the Mustangs, who broke away violently in surprise. Galland, making full use of the precious seconds he had gained, managed to get away.

Another fighter leader who survived was Colonel Josef 'Pips' Priller, *Kommodore* of JG 26 'Schlageter'. JG 26 had served on the Channel coast for a long time, and its pilots had built up enormous combat experience against the RAF and, more recently, the USAAF. Priller scored 101 victories, all of them in the west, and later became Inspector of Fighters in the west in place of Galland after the latter fell out with Hermann Göring.

But apart from the nucleus of surviving German aces – who were very, very good – the majority of *Luftwaffe* pilots in 1944 showed none of the skill and flair of two years earlier, although they continued to fight bravely and often suicidally.

As the year wore on, some of the men who flew the American escort fighters began to register formidable successes. One of them was Major George E. Preddy, who had arrived in England with the 352nd Fighter Group, flying P-47s, in July 1943. It was not until 1 December that he scored his first kill, but in the early months of 1944 his score began to mount rapidly. Later, the 352nd FG converted to Mustangs.

On 6 August 1944, Preddy was to lead the 352nd on a bomber escort mission to Germany. This came as bad news, because he and several other pilots had held a party of considerable proportions the night before, the Met. men having indicated that the weather would be too bad for operations. Preddy was still under the influence when he delivered his briefing, and at 32,000 feet on the outward leg he was sick all over the cockpit and himself. Then, as they approached the target area, the B-17s were attacked by enemy fighters. Preddy's combat report describes what happened next.

'We were escorting the lead combat wings of B-17s when thirty-plus Me 109s in formation came into the third box from the south. We were 1,000 feet above them so I led White Flight, consisting of Lieutenant Heyer, Lieutenant Doleac and myself, in astern of them. I opened fire on one near the rear of the formation from 300 yd dead astern and got many hits around the cockpit. The enemy aircraft went down inverted and in flames.

112

'At this time Lieutenant Doleac became lost while shooting down an Me 109 that had gotten on Lieutenant Heyer's tail. Lieutenant Heyer and I continued our attack and I drove up behind another enemy aircraft, getting hits around the wing roots, setting him on fire after a short burst. He went spinning down and the pilot baled out at 20,000 feet. I then saw Lieutenant Heyer on my right shooting down another enemy aircraft.

'The enemy formation stayed together taking practically no evasive action and tried to get back for an attack on the bombers who were off to the right. We continued with our attack on the rear end and I fired on another from close range. He went down smoking badly and I saw him begin to fall apart below us.

'At this time four other P-51s came in to help us with the attack. I fired at another 109, causing him to burn after a short burst. He spiralled down to the right in flames. The formation headed down in a left turn, keeping themselves together in rather close formation. I got a good burst into another one causing him to burn and spin down. The enemy aircraft were down to 5,000 ft now and one pulled off to the left. I was all alone with them now, so went after this single 109 before he could get on my tail. I got in an ineffective burst causing him to smoke a little. I pulled up into a steep climb to the left above him and he climbed after me. I pulled it in as tight as possible and climbed at about 150 miles an hour. The Hun opened fire on me but could not get enough deflection to do any damage. With my initial speed I slightly outclimbed him. He fell off to the left and I dropped down astern of him. He jettisoned his canopy as I fired a short burst getting many hits. As I pulled past, the pilot baled out at 7,000 ft.

'I lost contact with all friendly and enemy aircraft so headed home alone. CLAIM: Six (6) Me 109s.'

After this remarkable action Preddy went home on leave, returning to the 352nd FG in November. On Christmas Day, he was flying south-west of Coblenz when he sighted two Me 109s, which he chased and shot down; they were his 25th and 26th victims.

Soon afterwards, near Liège, he saw a low-flying Focke-Wulf 190 and went after it. The two aircraft ran into a storm of American anti-aircraft fire. Preddy tried to break away, but he was too late. Moments later, he was killed when his Mustang plunged into the ground.

In the late summer of 1944, Allied fighter pilots began to encounter increasing numbers of Messerschmitt Me 262 jets. With a top speed of 540 mph, the Me 262 was a good 100 mph faster than any Allied fighter in service at the time. It was armed with a battery of four 30-mm cannon, and although it suffered from a number of teething troubles – unreliable engines being one of them – it could have inflicted unacceptable losses on the USAAF's daylight bombers had it gone into full production as a fighter in the latter half of 1944. Hitler, however, was obsessed with the notion of using the Me 262 as a high-speed bomber, and it was in that role that the type entered *Luftwaffe* service in July 1944.

Jim Rosser, now a flight lieutenant and flying Spitfire XIVs with No 66 Squadron, was on patrol at 15,000 feet over Venlo in Holland one day in September 1944 when he sighted a 262 a few thousand feet lower down.

'I don't think anyone had actually managed to shoot down a 262 at that time, and I thought this was my big chance. I went down after him, flat out, but he saw me coming and opened the taps. Smoke trails streamed from his turbines and off he went; I hadn't a hope in hell of catching him, so I gave up and rejoined the formation.

'The incident had an interesting sequel. Years after the war, when I was stationed in Germany, I met a colonel in the Federal German *Luftwaffe*. We had a few drinks and got talking, and it turned out that he had flown 262s. We compared dates, places and times, and by one of those extraordinary coincidences it turned out that he had almost certainly been the pilot of "my" 262. He said that if I had kept after him, it was on the cards I would have got him. His fuel was very low, and he couldn't have maintained full throttle for more than half a minute. But there it was; I got shot down near Arnhem a few days later, so I never did get another chance to have a crack at a jet.'

Meanwhile, in August 1944, sufficient numbers of a new German jet aircraft type – the Arado Ar 234 bomber – had become available to permit the release of some Me 262s to form a fighter unit at Lechfeld, near Augsburg. It was originally commanded by Colonel Tierfelder, who was killed when his aircraft crashed in flames on one of the unit's first operational missions. His successor was Major Walter Nowotny, who, at the age of

23, was one of the *Luftwaffe's* top fighter pilots with a score of 258 kills, 255 of them achieved on the Eastern Front. By the end of October the *Kommando* Nowotny, as the unit had come to be known, was transferred to the airfields of Achmer and Hesepe near Osnabrück, astride the main American daylight bomber approach route.

Because of a shortage of adequately trained pilots and technical problems, the *Kommando* Nowotny was usually able to fly only three or four sorties a day against the enemy formations, yet in November 1944 the pilots destroyed 22 aircraft. By the end of the month, however, the unit had only three serviceable aircraft out of a total of 30 on strength, a rate of attrition accounted for mainly by accidents rather than enemy action.

On 8 November 1944, Walter Nowotny was the pilot of one of five Me 262s which took off to attack an American bomber formation. Operating from the 262 bases was now a very hazardous undertaking since the Allies had pinpointed their positions, and for several days they had been subjected to heavy attacks by fighter-bombers. Additional 20-mm flak batteries were brought up and organised into flak lanes, extending for two miles outwards from the ends of the main runways to provide a curtain of fire during the jet fighters' critical take-off and landing phases. For additional protection, a group of Focke-Wulf 190s was assigned to the air defence of Achmer and Hesepe.

On this November morning, in the operations room at Achmer, the German controllers followed the course of the air battle that developed at 30,000 feet over Germany. They heard Nowotny claim a victory, and also heard one of the other 262 pilots state that he was being shot down by the Mustangs. A few minutes later, Nowotny came on the air again to report that his port engine had failed and that he was coming in to make an emergency landing. Some time later, his 262 was sighted on the approach about four miles away from Achmer with wheels and flaps down and at least six Mustangs behind it. The observers on the ground saw Nowotny's undercarriage come up and the 262 go into a steep climbing turn on one engine. He had obviously decided to try and fight it out rather than land, which would have been suicide. A few seconds passed, then the watchers saw the 262 and its pursuers disappear behind a low hill. There was a dull explosion followed by a column of black smoke. The Mustangs climbed away pursued by scattered bursts of flak, leaving the wreckage of Nowotny's 262 scattered over a field near the village of Bremsche.

Soon after Nowotny's death, the jet fighter *Kommando* returned to Lechfeld for further training. Most of the pilots had only ten hours' experience on the 262, and the air battles of November had shown that not even the jet fighter's superior speed would compensate for the lack of experience when confronted with veteran Allied fighter pilots.

One of the latter was Captain Charles Yeager of the 357th Fighter Group, who on 6 November 1944 was leading a flight of Mustangs north of Osnabrück when three Me 262s were sighted, flying on an opposite course to the Mustangs and at two o'clock low. The Mustangs dived down from 10,000 feet and Yeager attacked the last jet in the trio, scoring some hits before the jets pulled away. A few moments later he sighted the 262s again, flying under an overcast, and fired a high deflection burst at the leader. Again he scored hits, and again the 262s used their superior speed to get away. Then, a few more minutes into his patrol, Yeager spotted another 262 approaching to land at an airfield. Braving intense flak, he dived down at 500 mph and fired a short burst into the 262's wing. The jet crash-landed short of the airfield, its wing shearing off.

A couple of weeks earlier, 'Chuck' Yeager had destroyed five Me 109s in a single sortie. He ended the war with eleven and a half confirmed victories, and later became famous for his transonic flights in the Bell X-1 series of rocket-powered research aircraft.

The fighter unit assigned to protect the Me bases at Achmer and Hesepe was III/JG 54, which was equipped with the 'long-nose' Focke-Wulf 190D-9, the latest and most powerful version of that famous fighter aircraft. III/JG 54 came under the operational command of JG 26, still commanded by 'Pips' Priller. The leader of III/JG 54 itself was another ace, Captain Robert 'Bazi' Weiss, an Austrian from Vienna. On 29 December 1944, Weiss and three other pilots were shot down and killed in a fight with Spitfires near their base.

Although the later versions of the Spitfire were a match for the Fw 190D-9, only one RAF fighter type stood a reasonable chance of catching the elusive Me 262s. This was the Hawker Tempest, the most powerful allied fighter to see action in World War Two. The first Tempest squadrons had been sent into combat in the summer of 1944, their task to protect London against the V-1 flying bombs, and 52 Tempest pilots had destroyed five or more of these pilotless jet-propelled aircraft. The top-scoring pilot of the V-1 offensive was Squadron Leader J. Berry, who destroyed 61 flying bombs; he was followed by Squadron Leader R. van Lierde, a Belgian pilot, who shot down 40, and Wing Commander Roland Beamont – who commanded the Tempest Wing, and who was to achieve fame after the war as a test pilot – with a score of 32.

In September 1944 five Tempest squadrons – Nos 3, 56, 80 and 274 RAF, and No 486 RNZAF – were deployed to northwest Europe in support of the Allied forces advancing through Belgium and Holland. From Brussels, the Tempests moved up to Volkel, in Holland, where they formed No 122 Wing. This was commanded by Group Captain P.G. Jameson, DSO – the same officer who had taken the Hurricanes of No 46 Squadron to Norway in May 1940 and who had narrowly escaped with his life when the carrier HMS *Glorious* was sunk. For Jameson, the wheel had turned full circle.

Several of the Tempest pilots were already aces. Squadron Leader Bob Spurdle, a New Zealander who commanded No 80 Squadron, had destroyed eight enemy aircraft, probably destroyed four more, and damaged at least fifteen; another New Zealander, Squadron Leader Evan 'Rosie' Mackie, who assumed command of No 80 Squadron in December, already had fifteen enemy aircraft to his credit, and celebrated his arrival by shooting down an Fw 190 on 24 December. His final score was to rise to 21.

The most successful Tempest pilot of all, however, was an American. Squadron Leader D.C. Fairbanks had joined the RCAF in the summer of 1941, and had completed a tour of operations flying Spitfires with No 501 Squadron early in 1944 before joining No 274 Squadron as a flight commander in time to take part in the V-1 battle. Fairbanks, who had one victory to his credit during his Spitfire days, destroyed at least eleven enemy aircraft while flying Tempests. His outstanding period came during the early weeks of 1945. On 4 January he shot down an Fw 190, after which he was awarded a DFC, and on the 14th he claimed another Fw 190 and an Me 109. On the 23rd he destroyed a Ju 52 transport, together with one Ju 88 destroyed and one damaged on the ground, and the next day he claimed a second Ju 52 on the ground. On 11 February he shot down an Me 262, damaging another on the 14th, and two days later he claimed a pair of Me 109s. On 22 February he shot down a pair of Fw 190D-9s, followed by a third on the 24th. His luck ran out over Rheine on the following day, when his section of six Tempests was bounced by Focke-Wulfs; he was shot down and taken prisoner.

Close behind Fairbanks came Squadron Leader Warren Schrader, a New Zealander who was posted to command No 486 Squadron early in 1945. Schrader had 2½ earlier victories to his credit, and since arriving in No 122 Wing he had destroyed four Fw 190s and an Me 109. During fierce fighting on 29 April, 1945, Schrader destroyed three Me 109s and shared a fourth. Soon afterwards, he was promoted wing commander and took command of No 616 Squadron, which had just arrived at Fassberg with Gloster Meteor F.3 jet fighters. Schrader rounded off his fighting career on 3 May by destroying an Me 109 and a He 111 on the ground and damaging a Ju 87, also on the ground. In air combat he had a total of eleven and a half kills, nine of them while flying Tempests.

The *Luftwaffe*, meanwhile, had continued to fight hard, with ever-dwindling resources, during those tumultuous weeks of 1945. Out of the *Kommando* Nowotny the nucleus of a new jet fighter unit had been born: JG 7 'Hindenburg', commanded by Colonel Johannes 'Macki' Steinhoff. Although JG 7 comprised three groups, only one of these – III/JG 7 – made real and continual contact with the enemy, hopping from one base to another, always under threat of air attack. During the last week of February 1945, using a combination of 30-mm cannon and R4M air-to-air rockets, the pilots of III/JG 7 destroyed no fewer than 45 four-engined American bombers and fifteen of their escorting fighters for the loss of only four 262s. There were further successes during March, although the 262s' loss rate continued to climb. On one occasion on 24 March, five 262s were shot down by Mustangs and Thunderbolts escorting bombers to Berlin. Despite what was rapidly becoming a serious rate of attrition, on 4 April JG 7 launched 49 Me 262s against a formation of American bombers over Nordhausen, destroying ten and claiming fifteen probably destroyed.

Meanwhile, in January 1945, permission had at last been granted for the formation of a new Me 262 fighter unit commanded by Lieutenant-General Adolf Galland. By the beginning of March Galland had recruited 45 pilots, all of them highly experienced. They included Macki Steinhoff, who turned over command of JG 7 to Major Theodor Weissenberger – an ace with 208 victories, 175 of them scored in the east – and walked out to join Galland without waiting for any authority from his superiors.

Steinhoff was without doubt one of the *Luftwaffe*'s most experienced fighter pilots, having amassed 176 confirmed victories since shooting down his first enemy aircraft – the RAF Wellington near Heligoland on 18 December 1939. As Galland's second-in-command of *Jagdverband* 44, as the Me 262 unit was known, he fought on until almost the last day of the war, when his jet fighter crashed in flames. He survived, despite appalling burns, and in the 1960s rose to be Inspector-General of the Federal German *Luftwaffe*.

Other talented and much-decorated pilots who flew Me 262s alongside Galland and Steinhoff included Colonel Gordon Gollob, who had gained 160 victories since the day, four and a half years earlier, when he had fought in his Me 110 against RAF Spitfires over the Farne Islands during the disastrous raid of 15 August 1940.

Then there was Colonel Heinz Bär, who had fought alongside Mölders in the Battles of France and Britain. He had fought in Russia, and over Malta and North Africa, and by April 1944 his score had reached 200. He gained a further four victories before joining JV 44, and scored a record sixteen kills while flying Me 262s, making him the top-scoring German jet pilot. In shooting down British and American aircraft, he was second only to Hans-Jochen Marseille. He survived those last hectic battles over Europe, only to die in an air crash in April 1957.

Such were the men who fought against hopeless odds in the twilight of the Third Reich.

On 7 April 1945, Theodor Weissenberger's JG 7 destroyed 28 Mustangs and Thunderbolts which were escorting American bombers over Germany.

On that same day, other Allied fighters sent 183 piston-engined Focke-Wulfs and Messerschmitts to destruction in what was the last series of major air battles in the European war.

Three days later, over 1,000 American bombers shattered the Me 262 bases with a rain of high explosive. The 262s shot down ten of the bombers, but with their bases devastated the jet units were broken up and scattered piecemeal. In the last days of April the remnants of *Jagdverband* 44 moved south to Salzburg, where the jets were grounded through lack of fuel. On 3 May, the surviving Messerschmitts were destroyed by the German ground crews.

Within hours, American tanks were rolling across the airfield.

CHAPTER TEN

The Eastern War, 1941–45

In the bitter air fighting that raged over the Eastern Front between 1941 and 1945, many Soviet fighter pilots achieved high scores. Foremost among them was Ivan Nikitich Kozhedub, who with 62 confirmed victories was the top-scoring Allied ace. But men such as Kozhedub achieved most of their success during and after the great air battles fought over the Kursk Salient in the summer of 1943, when the Soviet fighter regiments at last had aircraft which were as good as, and in some cases better than, their German adversaries.

For the pilots who fought to stem the German onslaught in the weeks that followed the attack of 22 June 1941, it was a different story. Their aircraft were outclassed, their tactics hopeless, their experience lacking, and as a result they suffered appalling losses. Most of the Red Air Force's fighter units were still equipped with I-15 and I-16 aircraft, which had been considered first-class when they had fought on the Republican side during the Spanish Civil War, but which now proved no match for the *Luftwaffe*'s Messerschmitt 109s and 110s. Their brave endeavours to protect the bomber formations that were thrown into battle against the advancing German panzer divisions cost them dearly, and the sheer hopelessness of their position sometimes led to desperate tactics. On the morning of 22 June, for example, Lieutenant Dmitri V. Kokorev of the 124th Air Regiment, having exhausted his ammunition in a dogfight, deliberately manoeuvred his I-16 to ram an Me 110, destroying both aircraft. Lieutenants P.S. Ryabtsev and A.S. Danilov of the 123rd Air Regiment also made ramming attacks that day, as did First Lieutenant Ivanov of the 46th Air Regiment. Ivanov alone survived.

Soviet fighter regiments equipped with more modern types fared somewhat better, although they too suffered from sadly inferior tactics. At the end of 1940 three new fighter types were just entering production: the first of these was the Yak-1 *Krasavyets* (Beauty), which made its first public appearance at an air display on 7 November 1940. It was Alexander S. Yakovlev's first fighter design, and it earned him the Order of Lenin, the gift of a Zis car and a prize of 100,000 roubles. The fighter was powered by a 1,100 hp M-105PA engine and carried an armament of one 20-mm cannon and two 7.62-mm machine-guns. It was of mixed construction, fabric and plywood covered; it was simple to build and service, and a delight to fly. Maximum speed was 360 mph.

The second type, the MiG-1, was the fruit of collaboration between the two aero engineers Artem I.Mikoyan and Mikhail I. Guryevitch, who were later to be responsible for the famous MiG-15 jet fighter. Heavier than the Yak-1, it was powered by a 1,350 hp engine that gave it a maximum speed of 380 mph at 23,000 feet; it carried an armament of two 7.62-mm and one 12.7-mm machine-guns. The third fighter, the LaGG-3, took its name from the initials of the three engineers who conceived it: Lavochkin, Gorbunov and Gudkov. It was a remarkable little aircraft, built entirely of wood and armed with one 20-mm cannon and three machine-guns. Its top speed was 345 mph.

Only 100 MiG-1 fighters were built before production switched to a modified version, the MiG-3, more than 1,300 of which were built in the first half of 1941. In the hands of skilled pilots it was a formidable adversary, and in action it soon began to score numerous successes. Two units that were equipped with it at the time of the German invasion were the 401st and 402nd Fighter Regiments, commanded respectively by Colonel Stepan Suprun and Colonel Pyotr Stefanovsky. The unusual thing about both these fighter regiments was that their flying personnel were almost all test pilots, both civil and military, and their collective experience soon paid dividends.

The 401st Fighter Regiment went into action on 1 July 1941, and on that first day destroyed four Me 109s for the loss of one of their own number. During the next two days the regiment shot down eight enemy aircraft for no loss, but the record was marred on the 4th when three MiGs were shot down by flak while strafing an enemy armoured column. One of the pilots who failed to return was Stepan Suprun, whose aircraft was hit and burst into flames as it climbed away from an attack. Suprun, who had been born in the United States, had been made a Hero of the Soviet Union during the Soviet-Japanese war on the Manchurian border in the summer of 1938; on 22 July 1941 he was posthumously awarded a second HSU gold star.

Suprun's place as commander of the 401st Fighter Regiment was taken by Vladimir V. Kokkinaki, a famous pilot who had made several record-breaking intercontinental flights before the war and who was later to test Russia's early jet fighters. By the beginning of October the 401st, which was based at Borisov, near Minsk, had 54 victories to its credit, and a close rivalry existed between this unit and the 402nd, based at Idritsa. The 402nd first saw action on 3 July 1941 and destroyed six enemy aircraft, followed by six more the next day. The 402nd's primary task was close support and low-level reconnaissance, and its pilots had orders to avoid combat if possible – but the regiment's adjutant, Major K.A. Gruzdev, devised tactics to bring the enemy to battle. These involved a steep spiral climb to between 15,000 and 18,000 feet, where the MiG-3 enjoyed a performance advantage over the Me 109. The German pilots almost always followed the spiral, doubtless believing that they were chasing a novice instead of an aerobatic champion, which Gruzdev had been before the war. They discovered their mistake too late when Gruzdev stall-turned out of the climb and shot them down. By the end of 1941, this talented pilot had nineteen confirmed victories to his credit.

On the southern front, where the German armies were thrusting towards the Crimea, one MiG-3 unit which distinguished itself from the beginning was the 55th Fighter Regiment, commanded by Lieutenant-Colonel Vladimir P. Ivanov. Many pilots who were to become Russia's leading air aces saw their first combats with the 55th; foremost among them was Aleksandr I. Pokryshkin, who was to survive the war as the second-ranking Soviet ace with 59 victories. It was Pokryshkin who, more than any other pilot, developed the air fighting tactics that were to become standard throughout Soviet Fighter Aviation from 1943–45. Like the top-scorer, Ivan Kozhedub, Alexsandr Pokryshkin was to be awarded the HSU three times before the war ended, and was to reach high rank in the post-war Soviet Air Force.

In the Moscow sector, the most successful MiG-3 unit during the first months of the war was the 34th Fighter Regiment, commanded by Major L.G. Rybkin and based at Vnukovo. The top-scorer in 1941 was Lieutenant Stepan I. Platov, with twenty victories, followed by Lieutenants N.E. Tarankantchikov with ten and Semyon D. Baykov with nine. Other units assigned to the air defence of Moscow were equipped with Yak-1s. One of them was the 177th Fighter Air Regiment, and on the night of 7 August a pilot with this unit, 2nd Lt V.V. Talalikhin, made a daring night attack on a Ju 88 which was bombing the capital. Having exhausted all his ammunition, Talalikhin rammed the enemy aircraft and then took to his parachute. He destroyed four more aircraft before being killed in an air battle on 27 October 1941.

Another Yak-1 unit was the 69th Fighter Air Regiment, which was based at Odessa on the Black Sea and was commanded by Lieutenant-Colonel L.L. Shestakov. The 69th's war began in August 1941, when the Germans launched a major offensive on the Southern Front. The regiment was under-strength in terms of both manpower and aircraft, and during the air battles over Odessa the Russian pilots each flew four or five sorties a day. On 9 August, led by Shestakov, they engaged a formation of twelve Me 109s and destroyed nine of them without loss. During the next two and a half years, before the Germans were driven from the Crimea, twelve of the 69th's pilots were made Heroes of the Soviet Union; Shestakov himself flew 200 combat sorties and took part in 32 air battles, shooting down fifteen enemy aircraft. He was shot down and killed in the course of a dogfight near Proskurov on 13 March, 1944.

On the Northern Front, many Russian fighter units were equipped with ex-RAF Hawker Hurricanes and American Curtiss P-40 Tomahawks, both of which were shipped to Russia in substantial numbers soon after the German attack developed.

One such unit was the 72nd (Naval) Fighter Air Regiment, commanded by Lieutenant-Commander Boris F. Safonov. The war on the Murmansk Front intensified in the spring of 1942, as the *Luftwaffe* made determined attempts to destroy the Allied convoys that were bringing supplies to Russia via the northern route, and fierce air battles took place between Russian fighters and the Germans over the Kola inlet. In the course of these battles, Boris Safonov's score rose to 22 enemy aircraft destroyed and by May 1942 he had twice been awarded the HSU, the first pilot to achieve this double distinction during the war.

The unserviceability rate among the 72nd's P-40s was high, and when the fighters were ordered to provide air cover for the incoming convoy PQ 16 on 30 May 1942, only four aircraft could be made airworthy. The convoy, which was 60 miles offshore, was being savagely attacked by 40 German bombers escorted by Me 109s of the *Luftwaffe*'s JG 5 Polar Wing, and the four Russian fighters, led by Safonov, raced up to intercept. The other three P-40s were flown by Lieutenants Kukharenko, Pokrovsky and Orlov; the first was compelled to return to base soon after take-off with engine trouble, reducing the fighter force to three machines. In spite of the formidable odds, the Russians did not hesitate to attack; Pokrovsky and Orlov shot down a Junkers Ju 88 apiece and Safonov got two. He had just damaged a third when he radioed that his engine had been hit and that he would have to ditch. The crew of a Russian destroyer, escorting the convoy, saw him glide down and hit the sea about two miles away. The warship raced to the spot but Safonov had gone, dragged down into the icy depths of the Barents Sea inside his aircraft. His final score was 25 enemy aircraft destroyed.

The air battles that accompanied the German offensive towards the Caucasus oil-fields in the summer of 1942 produced a crop of Soviet fighter aces. One of them was First Lieutenant Mikhail D. Baranov, a flight commander with the 183rd Fighter Air Regiment. On 6 August, leading a patrol of four Yak-1s over the river Don, he encountered a formation of enemy bombers escorted by 25 fighters. Baranov attacked, shooting down an Me 109 on his first pass, and then engaged the bombers, damaging one so badly that it crash-landed behind the Russian lines. Looking round, he saw that the Messerschmitts were attacking some Russian I1-2 Shturmovik ground attack aircraft; he dived down and destroyed a 109, and then, with all his ammunition gone, he sliced off another 109's tail with his wing before baling out. Baranov went on to score a total of 24 victories before his death in action in 1943.

During the German push towards Stalingrad, in August 1942, some Soviet fighter regiments began to re-equip with the latest Russian fighter type, the Lavochkin La-5, which was developed from the LaGG-3. Towards the end of 1941, Semyon A. Lavochkin had fitted a standard LaGG-3 airframe with a 1,600 hp Shvetsov M-82A radial engine, and during flight testing the type was found to be 30 mph faster than the Messerschmitt Me 109F. The improved fighter, designated La-5, was extremely promising and was ordered into quantity production. The aircraft soon lived up to its promise: on 20 August, the 287th Fighter Air Division (Colonel S.P. Danilin) arrived with its La-5s to reinforce the 8th Air Army on the Stalingrad Front, and in just under a month its pilots destroyed 97 enemy aircraft in the course of 299 engagements.

Although Russian fighter tactics were by now greatly improved, many Russian pilots showed great reluctance to break off an engagement and return to base when their ammunition was exhausted, and ramming tactics continued to be widely employed. On 8 September 1942, for example, a young pilot of the 520th Fighter Air Regiment, Sergeant B.M. Gomolko, shot down a German bomber and then deliberately rammed another after his ammunition ran out. Gomolko baled out, and as he was descending under his parachute he saw the crew of a shot-down enemy bomber also floating earthwards close by. Gomolko landed, shot one of the Germans who tried to run away, and took the other two prisoner. Gomolko was later commissioned and awarded the Order of Lenin.

One of the highest-scoring Soviet fighter pilots during the battles over the River Volga was Flight Sergeant Vladimir Lavrinenkov, an La-5 pilot with the 287th Air Division, who opened his score by shooting down two Ju 87s in September. A month later, his tally had risen to sixteen. He ended the war with 35 victories, having been commissioned and twice awarded the HSU. Another top-scoring La-5 pilot, in the same regiment as Lavrinenkov, was Aleksei V. Alelyukhin, who went on to destroy 40 enemy aircraft and who also received the HSU twice.

The winter of 1942-3 showed that Russian fighter pilots could match, and often outfight, their German counterparts. The days when *Luftwaffe* aces could notch up fantastic scores against inexperienced, poorly-trained enemies were gone forever; and now, in the early weeks of 1943, Russian fighter squadrons everywhere along the 1,200-mile front were beginning to receive equipment that was more than a match for the Me 109, and which were capable of meeting the latest Focke-Wulf 190s on equal terms. Apart from the La-5, there was the Yakovlev Yak-9, which was a progressive development of the Yak-1. A heavy fighter, the Yak-9 – which was to be built in greater numbers than any other Russian fighter – could also be used in the fighter-bomber and reconnaissance roles, and one version armed with a 37-mm cannon was effective against armour.

By the middle of November 1942, one-quarter of the Soviet Air Force's fighting strength had been assembled on the Stalingrad Front in preparation for the massive Soviet counter-offensive, which began on 20 November 1942, and ended with the utter destruction of the German Sixth Army at the end of January 1943. During this period some Russian fighter pilots joined the ranks of the aces with unexpected ease, wreaking fearful slaughter on the lumbering transport aircraft that were making desperate attempts to supply the tens of thousands of German troops trapped in the Stalingrad pocket. On 9 January 1943, for example, eighteen pilots of the 235th Fighter Air Division attacked sixteen Ju 52 transports flying into Stalingrad; nine Junkers went down on the first firing pass, five of them in flames and the other four to make forced landings. The remaining seven Ju 52s tried to turn back, but the fighters pursued them and destroyed six more.

The battle for Stalingrad was a major turning point in the war on the Eastern Front, but the greatest was the Battle of Kursk, which took place in the summer of 1943. The German offensive at Kursk was to be their last, and it was broken in eight days. Overhead, massive formations of aircraft – as many as 500 at a time – locked in combat. In 76 major air battles which took place during the first day, the Russians shot down 106 enemy aircraft and lost 98 of their own. It was during the Kursk battle that Ivan Kozhedub scored his first victories, opening a record that would end with his 62nd victim in the sky over Berlin nearly two years later.

In the fierce air fighting over Kursk, one exploit stood out above all others. On 6 July, Guards Lieutenant Aleksei K. Gorovets, flying a Yak-9, was returning alone from a mission when he sighted a formation of twenty Ju 87 Stukas heading for the Russian lines. Using cloud cover to good advantage, Gorovets stalked the enemy formation until he was right on top of it, then he dived on the rearmost flight of dive-bombers. Three Stukas fell in flames before the startled Germans knew what was happening, and in the next few minutes the Russian pilot pressed home attack after attack, destroying six more bombers before he was fatally wounded by return fire. He was made a posthumous HSU.

The successful Soviet counter-attack at Kursk, followed by the recapture of Orel and Kharkov, created favourable conditions for the development of a general offensive on the southern wing of the Soviet–German front. The Soviet Supreme Command decided to free the entire left bank of the Dnieper, subsequently pushing on across the river and establishing a firm bridgehead on the opposite bank. The Russian offensive opened on 26 August 1943, supported by some 600 aircraft of the 16th Air Army, and the ensuing air battle produced some noteworthy exploits. On 24 September, for instance, Colonel Nikolai Varchuk, commander of the 737th Fighter Air Regiment and already an HSU, was leading a group of Yak-9s on a ground attack escort mission when he sighted 40 German bombers, escorted by fifteen Fw 190s, heading towards the Russian lines. Ordering the rest of his group to continue with their escort mission, Varchuk broke away with his wingman and attacked the bombers, shooting one down. As he pulled away from his attack, Varchuk was engaged by two Focke-Wulfs; he out-manoeuvred them and destroyed both in a series of determined head-on passes.

One Russian pilot who began his rise to fame in October 1943, as the Germans strove to dislodge the Russians from their bridgehead on the right bank of the Dnieper, was Lieutenant Kirill A. Yevstgneyev, a flight commander with the 240th Fighter Air Regiment. In the course of nine dogfights he destroyed twelve enemy aircraft, and his score continued to rise steadily during the months that followed. He was twice made a Hero of the Soviet Union, and by the end of the war he had flown 300 combat sorties, taken part in 120 air battles and shot down 56 enemy aircraft.

To support their offensive across the Dnieper, the Russians threw almost the whole of their fighter forces into ground-attack operations, at the same time reserving some fighter regiments to escort the transport squadrons which, when the spring thaw rendered the roads impassable, air-lifted supplies of food, ammunition and fuel to the advancing troops. In seventeen days, the Li-2 transport aircraft (the Russian version of the Douglas C-47 Dakota) flew 4,817 sorties, carrying 670 tons of fuel and supplies and over 5,000 men, reinforcements on the way out and wounded on the way back. It was a vital task, and one which could not have succeeded without strong fighter escort, for the *Luftwaffe* was still active on the Dnieper Front.

One unit tasked with fighter escort was the 866th Fighter Air Regiment, which was equipped with La-5s and was commanded by Captain Aleksandr I. Koldunov. Early in April 1944, a mechanised cavalry group broke through deep into the enemy's rear and found itself surrounded. Six Li-2s were detailed to ferry in supplies so that the group could hold on until the main body of troops arrived, and six La-5s of the 866th, led by Koldunov, were detailed to escort them. Over the front line, the Russian formation was engaged by twelve Fw 190s. Koldunov took on the German leader in a head-on attack; at the last moment, when a collision seemed inevitable, the German lost his nerve and broke away, exposing his belly to Koldunov's fire. The 190 went down in flames. Koldunov immediately engaged a second 190 and shot that down too. It was his 22nd victory. The La-5s escorted the transports until the latter had made their drops, then escorted them safely back to base. Koldunov was made a Hero of the Soviet Union in August 1944; by the end of the war he had been awarded a second gold star and his score had risen to 46. (His victories in the air were actually 36; the Russians, like the Germans, included aircraft destroyed on the ground in their tally of kills.)

In June 1944, with Soviet forces advancing westward from the Dnieper and the Crimea liberated, the Russians went on the offensive on the Northern Front, pressing hard against German and Finnish forces in Karelia. In this sector, which was densely forested and studded with lakes, there were few forward airstrips suitable for fighter operation, and so the advancing ground forces had only limited fighter support. The fighter regiments that were crammed into the few available forward strips flew intensively, the pilots making five or six sorties daily. Many fighter pilots distinguished themselves during this campaign. They included Major Andrei V. Chirkov, commander of the 196th Fighter Air Regiment, who on 28 June engaged three Me 109s, shot one down and forced the others to flee; he ended the war with a score of 26. Then there was 2nd Lieutenant Dmitri Yermakov of the 159th Fighter Air Regiment, who shot down eight enemy aircraft in as many days; Lieutenant Vladimir Serov, who also destroyed eight aircraft and who was to end the war with a score of 26; and Major Piotr A. Pokryshev of the 275th Fighter Air Division, whose score during the Karelian campaign rose to twenty. In all, 26 pilots of the 275th Air Division became Heroes of the Soviet Union in June 1944.

The main Soviet objective, in the summer of 1944, was the destruction of the German Army Group Centre. Centred on Minsk, this Army Group, which was under the command of Field Marshal Model, comprised the 2nd, 4th and 9th Armies and the 3rd Panzer Army: a total of 50 divisions, with 1,000 tanks and 1,200,000 men. For air support, the *Luftwaffe* had assembled some 1,400 combat aircraft. The destruction of Army Group Centre would not only result in the expulsion of German forces from Russian soil; the Army Group was defending what amounted to a broad highway that led into the heart of central Europe, and if Model's forces were smashed that highway would be left wide open. In readiness for the offensive, the Russians assembled over two and a half million men on four fronts, stretching in a great arc from the Baltic to the Dnieper.

The great Russian offensive opened on 22 June, 1944 – three years to the day after the Wehrmacht smashed into the Soviet Union – and the weeks that followed were marked by some of the bloodiest air fighting of the war.

In the northern Ukraine, the main Soviet thrust was directed towards Lvov, which was held by a mixture of German and Hungarian forces. In this sector, fighter support was provided by the 7th Fighter Air Corps; one of its units, the 9th Guards Fighter Division, was commanded by Aleksandr Pokryshkin and was equipped with American-built Bell P-39 Airacobras, aircraft which had been no match for the Japanese Zero fighters in the Pacific Theatre. The Russians, on the other hand, took to the American fighter and had considerable success with it.

On 13 July 1944, Pokryshkin and two of his flight commanders, Captain Grigorii Rechkalov and Lieutenant Andrei Trud, were each leading a flight of four Airacobras when they encountered a formation of about 40 Stukas and Henschel 129 assault aircraft, escorted by eight Fw 190s. While Trud's flight took on the fighters, Pokryshkin and Rechkalov attacked the bombers, which immediately formed a defensive circle. Together with his two wingmen, Lieutenants Golubev and Zherdev, Pokryshkin gained height and then dived into the middle of the circle, turning with the Stukas and opening fire when the opportunity presented itself. He quickly shot down one Ju 87, then found himself in trouble when a Focke-Wulf dropped into the mêlée and got his tail. Golubev shouted a warning over the radio and tried to get into position to open fire, but dared not do so for fear of hitting his leader. The German's cannon punched a hole in Pokryshkin's starboard wing, and the ace's career might have ended right there if Zherdev had not managed to shoot down the German with a lucky deflection shot. Despite the damage to his aircraft, Pokryshkin went on to shoot down two more Stukas; his pilots destroyed six more.

Soon afterwards, Aleksandr Pokryshkin received the third of his gold stars. Of the other pilots engaged in this action, Rechkalov rose to be third-ranking Soviet ace with 58 victories; Golubev's score was 39 and Trud's 24. There is no record of what became of Zherdev.

Another Soviet ace who increased his score in the summer of 1944 was Captain Aleksandr Klubov, who had first seen combat in Pokryshkin's regiment in the summer of 1941–2. Klubov had a reputation for remaining extremely calm, even under the most hectic conditions. On one occasion, he set off on a lone reconnaissance mission and became overdue. Pokryshkin, who had stayed behind at base, called him repeatedly over the radio and eventually made contact, wanting to know what was happening. 'I'm in the middle of a scrap,' was the laconic reply. As dusk was falling, Klubov's aircraft appeared over the airfield, behaving very erratically. It was pitching violently, as though on a switchback. Klubov made his approach, gunning the engine from time to time and brought the fighter down on its belly with a terrific crash. He climbed from the cockpit, unhurt, as the other pilots came running up. The aircraft was a complete wreck, riddled from end to end with cannon shell and machine-gun bullet holes. Klubov explained that he had been attacked by six Me 109s and that he had shot down two of them before a third had shot away his elevator controls. Nevertheless, he had managed to make his escape and had kept the aircraft flying by careful use of the throttle, cramming on power to bring the nose up when the fighter showed signs of going into a dive. A lesser pilot would have baled out.

During a five-day period in August 1944, while flying in support of German forces that were pushing into Romania, Aleksandr Klubov destroyed nine enemy aircraft. During his combat career, which lasted until his death in action in November 1944, he flew 457 sorties and gained 31 victories. He was posthumously awarded a second gold star.

While the Russians advanced to the Vistula and established a series of bridgeheads on the west bank of the river, Soviet forces were pushing the Germans steadily back through Latvia and Estonia. By the end of the year, Estonia had been liberated completely and the German forces that remained in Latvia were penned up in the north-west corner of the country. They were still there when the Germans surrendered in May 1945. Ivan Kozhedub, already the leading scorer among the Russian fighter pilots, operated on this front during the autumn of 1944. His regiment was a special unit, and was liable to be sent anywhere on the front where the fighting was toughest. It was equipped with the new Lavochkin La-7, basically similar to the La-5 but with aerodynamic improvements that gave it a better combat performance.

In September, the Russians occupied Romania and Bulgaria. The following month, they captured Belgrade and moved north-westwards into Hungary to begin a winter offensive against the German and Hungarian armies which were still putting up a stiff resistance. By mid-December, 180,000 German and Hungarian troops were besieged in Budapest. At the turn of the year, the front ran from Yugoslavia to the Baltic, cutting across Poland and Czechoslovakia and running along the border of

East Prussia. The stage was now set for the great offensive of 1945. For the final thrust that would take them into Germany the Russians had assembled nearly 5,000,000 men, twice as many as the opposing Germans, divided among 45 field armies, eleven Guards armies, five shock armies and six tank armies. A vast air umbrella over the offensive would be provided by the 17,000 combat aircraft of thirteen air armies; they outnumbered the *Luftwaffe* on the Eastern Front by ten to one.

The *Luftwaffe* suffered terrible losses during those last weeks of the war in the east. Groups of bomb-carrying Focke-Wulfs and Messerschmitts were hurled against the advancing Russians in what amounted to suicide missions; they were mostly flown by inexperienced pilots who had been hastily converted from other types and who had had no time to become accustomed to flying high-performance fighter-bombers. Weighed down by their bombs, they were easy prey for the Russian fighters. On 18 January, six La-5s of the 9th Guards Fighter Air Regiment, commanded by Captain Pavel Golovachev, attacked a formation of 25 Fw 190s and shot down five of them; the remainder jettisoned their bombs and flew away westwards. The Russians suffered no losses. Golovachev, twice an HSU, had a score of 31 enemy aircraft destroyed when the war ended.

At the beginning of February 1945, with the Russians pushing towards Berlin, the Germans scraped together their last reserves of aircraft in a desperate attempt to gain air superiority over the Eastern Front. The German High Command still entertained hopes of concluding a separate armistice with the Western Allies; the goal now was to hold up the Soviet advance for as long as possible, in order to buy time. During the first two weeks of February the initiative sometimes passed to the Germans, as most of the Russian fighter airfields were unusable because of mud, but matters improved during the second half of the month and the *Luftwaffe*'s losses began to mount once more.

One of the last major air battles of the eastern war took place on 18 April, when 24 Yak-9s of the 43rd Fighter Air Regiment, led by First Lieutenant Ivan G. Kuznetsov, sighted 35 Fw 190s and Me 109s, all carrying bombs and heading for the front line. Using cloud cover to good advantage, the Russian pilots stalked the enemy for some distance and then pounced on them, scattering them and forcing them to jettison their bombs on their own ground forces. In the ensuing air battle Kuznetsov shot down four enemy aircraft, as did two other pilots, Ivan Chernenkov and Nikolai Gribkov.

During the final phases of the battle for Berlin, there were outbreaks of bitter air fighting over the shattered German capital. On 28 April, seven La-5 pilots of the 263rd Fighter Air Regiment attacked 25 Focke-Wulfs which were attempting to strike at Soviet troops. Second Lieutenant Nikolai Brodsky sliced through the enemy formation and shot down a 190, and was immediately attacked himself by six more. He escaped by pulling up into the clouds, then turned and dived clear to find another 190 in his sights, which he promptly shot down also. Captain Andrei Chetvertkov also destroyed two enemy aircraft in this battle, and altogether the Russians accounted for seven.

On that same day, Yak-9s of the 515th Fighter Air Regiment landed at Tempelhof airfield, within the perimeter of Berlin. Forty-eight hours later, Adolf Hitler committed suicide and the battle for Berlin entered its final hours.

Ironically, neither of Russia's top-scoring air aces was there to witness the final German surrender. Ivan Kozhedub had flown to Moscow a couple of days earlier to represent the air units of the First White Russian Front at the traditional May-Day Parade, while Aleksandr Pokryshkin's division had moved south to an airfield near Prague. The Czech capital was the last pocket of German resistance in the east; the garrison held out for a week after the fall of Berlin.

On 9 May, the day of the final German surrender in Prague, Major Viktor Golubev – one of Pokryshkin's pilots, and the sixteenth-ranking Soviet air ace – shot down a Messerschmitt 109 over the city. It was the last aircraft to be destroyed in air combat during the European war, and Golubev's thirty-eighth victory.

Even today, the story of Russia's fighter pilots and their exploits during World War Two remains relatively unknown outside the Soviet Union. Yet 203 of those pilots destroyed twenty or more enemy aircraft between June 1941 and May 1945 – a cumulative total of 5,324. It was no mean contribution to the Allied victory in the air.

CHAPTER ELEVEN

Battle for the Pacific.

In the months that followed the Japanese attack on Pearl Harbor in December 1941, the fighter aircraft that held the line for the United States was the Grumman F4F Wildcat. Powered by a Pratt & Whitney Twin Wasp radial engine and armed with four .50 calibre machine-guns, the tubby little Wildcat was the standard single-seat fighter in service with the US Navy and US Marine Corps at that time. Completely outclassed by the Imperial Japanese Navy's standard fighter, the Mitsubishi Zero, it fought valiantly against hopeless odds in those early months of the Pacific War, and many American aces scored their first victories while flying it.

The Wildcats first met the Japanese in action during the heroic defence of Wake Island in December 1941, shooting down nine Japanese aircraft before they were overwhelmed. The first kill by a carrier-based Wildcat pilot was scored by Lieutenant (jg) W.E. Rawie, who was strafing Japanese positions during an attack on the Japanese-held Marshall and Gilbert Islands by the aircraft carriers USS *Yorktown* and USS *Enterprise* on 1 February 1942 when he was attacked by two Mitsubishi A5M Claude fighters. He turned into them and shot one of them down as they went past.

A second US carrier strike was laid on later in the month, this time by the USS *Lexington* against Rabaul, the idea being to try and relieve growing Japanese pressure on Port Moresby in New Guinea. Part of *Lexington's* carrier air group was VF-3, a Wildcat squadron commanded by Lieutenant-Commander John S. Thach. An excellent shot and the US Navy's leading exponent of air tactics, Thach had developed a defensive manoeuvre which became known as the Thach Weave. This involved elements of two aircraft, with about 300 yards' spacing between each aircraft so that each pilot could watch his partner's tail. If a pilot was attacked from astern, he would break towards his partner, who would also break outwards towards the second pair. This pair would then break inwards in order to meet the threat head-on; the attacking aircraft would effectively be drawn into a trap. It proved an excellent tactical manoeuvre, and with modifications it is still used today.

Thach had insisted on his pilots constantly striving to improve their marksmanship, so that in February 1942 VF-3's gunnery record was probably the best in the US Navy. Their skill was to stand them in good stead, and compensated in part for the Wildcat's shortcomings. It was also appropriate that Thach himself had the privilege of scoring VF-3's first kill, a Kawanishi H6K Mavis reconnaissance flying boat which he shot down in flames 400 miles north-east of Rabaul. The Japanese crew made no attempt to abandon their aircraft and the gunners kept on firing until the Mavis exploded on the sea.

It was soon clear that the Japanese had remained at their posts long enough to alert their HQ on Rabaul to the presence of an American aircraft carrier. Late that afternoon, nine Mitsubishi G4M Betty bombers were seen approaching the USS *Lexington*. They were engaged by the carrier's combat air patrol (CAP) and the Wildcats shot down four of them, but the rest continued on course and bombed in formation from 11,000 feet. The bombing was accurate, but the carrier took evasive action and escaped damage. Then, as the Wildcats were preparing to land-on in order to refuel and re-arm, a second formation of nine Bettys was detected by the carrier's radar.

Only two Wildcats were in a position to intercept this second attack, and their pilots showed no hesitation. In the leading fighter, Lieutenant H. 'Butch' O'Hare ripped into the Japanese formation and sent down two Bettys in flames on his first pass. The Betty had an excellent range, but this had been achieved by saving weight at the expense of armour protection for the crew and fuel tanks; as a result, when the Betty was subjected to a determined attack it almost invariably went up like a torch. Turning back into the formation, O'Hare braved heavy defensive fire to destroy another bomber, quickly followed by two more. In just five minutes, he had become the US Navy's first air ace.

By this time, John Thach and other Wildcat pilots had arrived to join the fight, and they followed the surviving bombers for as long as their fuel permitted. Of the eighteen Japanese bombers that tried to attack *Lexington* that day, thirteen went blazing into the sea. For his personal exploit, Butch O'Hare was awarded the Congressional Medal of Honor. He went on to score a total of 12 kills before being killed in action during a strike on Gilbert Islands on 26 November 1943. He was then commanding Air Group 6 on the USS *Enterprise*.

On 7 August 1942, a division of United States Marines stormed ashore on Guadalcanal, in the Solomon Islands. For the Americans, it was the first step on the long journey back across the Pacific, a journey that would end almost exactly three years later with the nuclear destruction of Hiroshima and Nagasaki. One of the main American objectives in the invasion of Guadalcanal was to capture an airstrip which had been built there by the Japanese. The Marines went in and took it, and the land battle subsequently centred on the struggle to retain it. In one of the most tenacious and heroic actions of the Pacific War the Marines clung grimly to their positions around the strip, which they had named Henderson Field, and by 20 August it had been made sufficiently secure for the first US fighters to fly in.

They were the Wildcats of Marine Fighter Squadron VMF-223, led by Major John L. Smith, and they were followed by Major Robert E. Galer's VMF-224 a few days later. The day after their arrival on Guadalcanal, the pilots of VMF-223 intercepted six Zeros at 14,000 feet over the island, and Major Smith shot down one of them to score the squadron's first victory. The following afternoon the Japanese came again, this time with fifteen bombers escorted by twelve Zeros. All of VMF-223's serviceable Wildcats took off to intercept the enemy, and in the course of a savage air battle they destroyed sixteen Japanese aircraft for the loss of three Wildcats. John Smith and one of his flight commanders, Captain Marion E. Carl, each shot down three.

Day after day, while the ground forces strove desperately to hold the thin perimeter around Henderson Field, the Marine pilots went into action against the Japanese squadrons that were making determined attempts to wipe out the primitive airstrip. At the same time, Japanese warships shelled the base every night, and individual enemy aircraft carried out nuisance raids to ensure that the American pilots got little rest. As the weeks went by, malaria, dysentery and fatigue began to have a telling effect, yet the Americans, flying to the limits of their physical endurance, somehow managed to retain air superiority. By the time VMF-223 was relieved in October 1942, the pilots had destroyed 110 enemy aircraft; John Smith's score was 19, while his close rival Marion Carl had shot down 16. Major Robert E. Galer, of VMF-224, had chalked up 13 victories; both he and Smith were awarded the Congressional Medal of Honor. All three survived the war.

The replacement squadrons of Guadalcanal were VMF-121 and VMF-212. One of the former's pilots was Captain Joe Foss, a farm boy from South Dakota whose marksmanship – thanks to his father's tuition with rifle and shotgun – was superb. Foss rose to fame with incredible speed over Guadalcanal; by the middle of October he was averaging one victory a day, and by the end of the month three a day. On 23 and 25 October he destroyed a total of nine enemy aircraft, all of them Zeros. By the time VMF-121 left Guadalcanal in January 1943 its pilots had destroyed 123 Japanese aircraft for the loss of fourteen Wildcats. Joe Foss's personal score was 26, which made him the first American to equal the score of Eddie Rickenbacker, the leading American ace of World War One. His outstanding combat record earned Joseph J. Foss the Congressional Medal of Honor. He never flew in combat again (the American policy was that outstanding combat pilots who had been awarded the Congressional Medal of Honor should not be required to risk their lives in action again) and, after the war, he became Governor of South Dakota.

The exploits of Joe Foss tended to outshadow all others in the embattled sky over Guadalcanal. But in the hectic days of October and November 1942, when the Japanese were making their most determined attempts to recapture the island, the effective resistance of the American pilots was due in no small measure to the dedicated leadership of one man. He was Lieutenant-Colonel Harold W. Bauer, known throughout US Marine aviation as 'Indian Joe'.

Bauer was the commanding officer of VMF-212, which was based at Efate in the New Hebrides when the battle for Guadalcanal began. His initial task was to provide a pool of trained replacement Wildcat pilots for the two Marine squadrons already in action on the island, and before long he was making frequent visits to Guadalcanal himself, flying combat air patrols with the others. On 28 September, he destroyed an Aichi D3A Val dive bomber, his first victory, and on 3 October he claimed four Zeros, part of a Japanese fighter force which was escorting a large group of Betty bombers. He got four more enemy aircraft – all Vals – on 16 October, the day that he led his own VMF-212 into action on the island.

It was Bauer who instructed his Wildcat pilots to dogfight with the Zeros; this had been attempted earlier, with disastrous results because the Zero was more manoeuvrable than the Wildcat, but Bauer had shrewdly assessed that the Japanese must now be fielding more inexperienced replacement pilots. He was right, and in a big air battle on 23 October, 24 Wildcats and four US Army Air Corps P-39s took on a big formation of Betty and Zekes and shot down twenty fighters and two bombers. All the enemy aircraft fell in the vicinity of the airfield in clear view of the exhausted defenders, providing a massive boost to their morale.

On that day, Bauer was appointed Commander of Fighters on Guadalcanal. On 14 November, after shooting down another Zero – his eleventh victim – while providing top cover for US bombers which were attacking Japanese shipping off the island, he was himself hit and sent down into the sea. The other pilots saw him in his lifejacket, waving, and sent out a Grumman Duck amphibian to pick him up, but despite an intensive air and sea search Indian Joe Bauer was never found. He was posthumously awarded the Congressional Medal of Honor.

On 26 October 1942, US and Japanese naval forces – the latter covering and supporting a major land attack designed to seize Henderson Field – met head-on in a major engagement that was to become known as the Battle of Santa Cruz. It developed into a slogging match between carrier aircraft of the opposing sides, and in the fierce air battles one US Navy Wildcat pilot particularly distinguished himself. His name was Lieutenant Stanley W. Vejtasa, who destroyed no fewer than seven enemy torpedo-bombers in a single engagement. Vejtasa was then flying with VF-10 aboard the USS *Enterprise* and he already had three victories to his credit, gained during the Battle of the Coral Sea in May 1942. These kills were also claimed in a single fight, but the extraordinary thing was that Vejtasa notched them up while flying a Douglas SBD Dauntless dive-bomber from the USS *Yorktown*.

On 8 May, Vejtasa's SBD was one of a formation searching for Japanese aircraft carriers when the American bombers were bounced by about twenty Zeros. Two SBDs were soon shot down and the remainder formed a defensive circle, turning desperately and firing at the Zeros whenever the chance presented itself. The fight went on for forty minutes, and in that time Vejtasa shot down three of the Zeros. The fact that he applied for a transfer to fighters soon afterwards came as no surprise to anyone.

Another US Navy Wildcat pilot who distinguished himself by becoming an ace in one day was Lieutenant (jg) E.S. 'Scott' McCuskey of VF-42, which operated from the USS *Yorktown* during the Battle of Midway in June 1942. Sighting a formation of enemy torpedo-bombers heading for his carrier, he attacked the first wave head-on and sent three of them down in flames. He then turned in behind another three and damaged them before running out of ammunition. Later in the day, he destroyed two more torpedo-bombers. McCuskey was to survive the war with a score of thirteen confirmed kills.

The Battle of Midway cost the Imperial Japanese Navy four fast attack carriers – the ships that had launched the devastating strike on Pearl Harbor seven months earlier – as well as 258 aircraft and many of its most experienced naval pilots. It was a decisive defeat from which the Japanese were never to recover; it was Midway, more than any other action, that destroyed Japan's hopes of further expansion in the Pacific.

At this time, many of the leading pilots of the Imperial Japanese Navy were based at Lae, on the east coast of New Guinea, where their wing of Zero fighters was tasked with providing air support for Japanese bomber operations against Port Moresby. The Japanese, pushing through the Owen Stanley Mountains, were making ceaseless attempts to capture this vital objective, which was to serve as the springboard for an invasion of northern Australia, and were meeting fierce resistance from Australian and American troops. Lae was only 180 miles from Port Moresby, and day after day in that summer of 1942 the sky over the mountainous jungle terrain separating the two bases became the scene of bitter air battles as the Allies threw in all their resources to halt the Japanese advance. For the first time, the Zero squadrons began to sustain real losses in combat with fighters – mostly Bell B-39 Airacobras and Curtiss P-40 Tomahawks – flown superbly by US Army Air Corps and Royal Australian Air Force pilots.

Nevertheless, the Japanese managed to retain their overall air superiority for some time, and several pilots added to their scores in this theatre. Notable among them were Lieutenant-Commander Hiroyoshi Nishazawa, commanding the Lae Wing, who shot down twenty American aircraft in a month, who had 30 victories by November 1942 and whose score was eventually to reach 87; Saburo Sakai, who went on to claim a total of 64 victories; Toshio Ota with 34; and Junichi Sasai with 27. Their combined skill was considerable, but it was Sakai – perhaps the best-known of all the Japanese aces through his post-war writings – who was the real tactician among them, and who instilled the value of tactical air fighting into the Lae Wing's younger pilots.

His teaching paid dividends. On 23 April 1942, for example, Sakai's squadron engaged six B-26 Marauder bombers, fifteen P-40s and P-39s in the Port Moresby area and claimed the definite destruction of two bombers and six P-40s. The next day, the Zeros shot down six out of seven P-40s and also destroyed five B-26s on the ground in a strafing attack. Despite the ascendancy of the Zeros, the Allied bomber squadrons continued to press home their attacks on the Japanese bases with great courage, the twin-engined B-26 Marauders and B-25 Mitchells suffering heavy losses in the process. On 24 May the Zeros accounted for five out of six B-25s that bombed Lae, and a loss of this magnitude was by no means an exception.

But by the end of 1942, the aircraft that would turn the tide in the Allies' favour were beginning to reach the combat squadrons. The first was the heavy, powerful Chance Vought F4U Corsair, which entered service with Marine Fighter Squadron VMF-124 (The Checkerboards) at Camp Kearney, California, in September 1942. On 2 February 1943 the unit was declared combat-ready, and on 12 February twelve of its 22 Corsairs arrived at Henderson Field, Guadalcanal, to relieve the battle-weary Wildcats. On the following day they flew their first combat mission, escorting B-24 Liberator bombers in a raid on Bougainville in the Solomon Islands. The mission was uneventful and no enemy fighters were sighted, but on a similar mission on 14 February the American formation – which also included USAAF P-38s and P-40s – was attacked by about fifty Japanese fighters. The Corsair pilots, who were still inexperienced in handling their new aircraft – some had barely twenty hours' flying time on the type – were overwhelmed by superior numbers. In a matter of minutes the Zeros shot down two Liberators, two Corsairs, two P-40s and P-38s for the loss of four of their own number.

This disaster, which became known as the St Valentine's Day Massacre, was a humiliating start for VMF-124, but it made the pilots determined to master their new aircraft fully, and before long their successes began to mount. In the weeks that followed, VMF-124 destroyed 68 enemy aircraft for the loss of only eleven Corsairs and three pilots, an outstanding result by any standards.

One of VMF-124's best pilots during this period was Lieutenant Ken Walsh, who destroyed three Zeros on 1 April 1943 and three more on 13 May. A few days later, he added a seventh Zero and two Val dive-bombers to his score over Vella Lavella Island. Walsh eventually went on to attain a score of 21 enemy aircraft destroyed, and to be awarded the Congressional Medal of Honor. He served a full career in the USMC, retiring as a full colonel in the early 1960s.

The leading exponent of the Corsair – which by the autumn of 1943 equipped all the USMC's fighter squadrons – was Major Gregory 'Pappy' Boyington, who had flown for a short time with VMF-122 on Guadalcanal in April 1943. After this, he was given command of VMF-214, which was nicknamed the 'Black Sheep' squadron because it was made up of a group of casual, replacement and green pilots. Boyington soon welded the Black Sheep into shape, and took them into action in the Russell Islands in September 1943. On 16 September, the squadron fought a major air battle over Ballale; it was intercepting a formation of Japanese bombers when it was itself attacked by 50 Zeros, and in the dogfight that followed the Black Sheep destroyed twelve enemy aircraft, Boyington himself claiming five. This brought his score so far to eleven, for he had already gained six victories while flying with the American Volunteer Group in China during 1941–2.

On 17 December 1943, Boyington led the first Allied fighter sweep over the Japanese-held island of Rabaul, which was very heavily defended, and it was over this location, on 27 December, that he scored his 25th victory, his kills having mounted steadily in the interim. On 3 January 1944 he led his pilots over Rabaul again, and encountered twelve Zeros. Boyington shot down one of them, then dived down through broken cloud with his wingman, Lieutenant Ashmun, to attack another enemy formation. Boyington destroyed two more Zeros, but the odds were too great and both he and Ashmun were shot down in turn. Boyington managed to bale out and spent the rest of the war as a Japanese PoW, surviving to be liberated in 1945. With 28 victories, he was to remain the top-scoring USMC ace. He, too, was awarded the congressional Medal of Honor.

The third-ranking USMC ace, behind Boyington and Joe Foss, was First Lieutenant Robert M. Hanson. Unlike the other two, he scored all his 25 kills while flying the Corsair, and he was unique in that he destroyed twenty enemy aircraft in just six combat missions – an achievement that was not to be equalled by any other Allied pilot in World War Two. He went into combat late in 1943 with VMF-215, which was one of the Corsair units given the task of providing air support for amphibious landings by US Marines on the south coast of Bougainville.

On 1 November, while flying top cover with the rest of the squadron, Hanson spotted a formation of six Val dive-bombers about to attack the American landing ships. He broke away solo and went after them, shooting one down and forcing the rest to jettison their bombs. He claimed three more enemy aircraft on 3 November – being forced to ditch his aircraft near the US task force when his Corsair's engine was hit – and another on 17

December, by which time VMF-215 had moved to a forward airstrip on Bougainville itself.

On 14 January, 1944, VMF-215 was detailed to escort a force of B-25 medium bombers in a raid on Rabaul. The Americans were attacked by an estimated 70 enemy fighters, and in the wild dogfight that ensued Hanson was credited with the destruction of five of them, doubling his score. He claimed a further four Japanese aircraft over Rabaul in the next two days, and on 24 January, while escorting a formation of Grumman Avenger torpedo-bombers on a shipping strike, he shot down four more Zeros and possibly destroyed a fifth. The Japanese pilots had been stalking the American bomber formation with the aid of cloud cover, and such was the fury of Hanson's attack that the enemy's intentions were completely disrupted.

Two days later, Hanson destroyed three more Zeros on his fifth mission to Rabaul. His score now stood at 21. On 30 January, again while escorting an Avenger shipping strike, he claimed a further three Zeros. With Boyington and Foss now gone – the former to a PoW camp and the latter back to the United States – bets were laid as to whether Hanson would beat both their scores on his next mission to Rabaul, and so become the top Marine Corps ace.

The next trip to Rabaul was laid on for 3 February. Hanson, with three other Corsairs, set out on a fighter sweep over the island, eager for action, but found that Rabaul was covered by dense cloud. Disappointed, the Corsair pilots turned for home. On the way back, Hanson called his leader and asked for permission to strafe a lighthouse on Cape Alexander on the southern tip of New Ireland; it was used as an observation post and flak tower by the enemy. He received permission, and his colleagues watched as he dived down to make his strafing attack. Then, to their horror, they saw a puff of smoke as a shell struck his aircraft. A piece flew off the Corsair's wing. Hanson struggled to retain control and tried to ditch the stricken fighter, but at the last moment it cartwheeled across the waves and vanished below the surface. The others circled over the spot for a few minutes, but there was no sign of the pilot. On 1 August 1944, seven months after his death, Robert Hanson was awarded a posthumous Congressional Medal of Honor.

If the Corsair was a vital instrument in the success of the US Marine Corps' Pacific Island assaults, the fighter that eventually took the US Navy's air war to Japan was the Grumman F6F Hellcat, a logical development of the Wildcat with a much better performance. The Hellcat first flew in June 1942, and the first operational aircraft were delivered to VF-9 on the USS *Essex* in January 1943. The Hellcat's first operational sorties were flown on 31 August 1943, when aircraft of VF-5 (USS *Yorktown*) strafed Japanese positions on Marcus Island in the western Pacific.

It was a combination of the sturdy little Hellcat and exceptional flying skill that was to produce the US Navy's leading ace of World War Two, Commander David S. McCampbell. His road to the cockpit of a front-line naval fighter had been long and arduous; in fact, he had almost not made it. A graduate of the Annapolis Naval Academy, he had applied for flying training with the US Navy in 1936, only to be rejected on the grounds of defective eyesight. Determined not to be beaten, he went to a civilian doctor, who submitted him to searching tests and assured him that there was nothing wrong with his eyes at all. McCampbell went back to the Navy doctors, and six months later he was accepted for flight training. He was awarded his pilot's wings on 23 April 1938, but found to his dismay that – because the US Navy was oversubscribed with pilots at that time, and because his medical record still dogged him – he was confined to the role of deck landing officer.

McCampbell's big chance did not come until the spring of 1944, when he was promoted to command Air Group 15 on board the USS *Essex*, flying Hellcats. His first action came on 19 May, when, flying his 'personal' Hellcat – which he had named Monsoon Maiden – he led his group on a dawn fighter sweep over Marcus Island. This remote spot in the Pacific, about 1,000 miles from Japan, was used more or less as a training ground for air groups about to go into action among the islands to the south and was not very heavily defended, but on this occasion a Japanese anti-aircraft shell struck Monsoon Maiden, setting her belly fuel tank on fire and damaging the rear fuselage. McCampbell jettisoned the tank just in time, and despite the damage to his aircraft he remained over the island, directing the other fighters in attacks on Japanese positions. He got back to the carrier by the skin of his teeth, his main fuel tanks almost dry. Monsoon

Maiden was judged to be beyond repair and was shovelled over the side.

This mission earned McCampbell a Distinguished Flying Cross and the unqualified respect of his men. Shortly afterwards, flying a new Hellcat named The Minsi, McCampbell led Air Group 15 into action as part of US Navy Task Force 58's offensive against the Marianas, and on 11 June he scored his first victory as aircraft from TF 58's four fast carrier task groups were pounding Japanese airfields and coastal defensive positions in preparation for the US landings on the islands. Sighting a lone Zero over Pagan Island, McCampbell overhauled it and shot it down in flames.

It had been an easy victory, for the Japanese pilot had taken no evasive action. But there was nothing easy about McCampbell's air combats that took place on 19 June 1944, when carrier fighters of TF 58 took part in the greatest and most concentrated air battle of all time. In a day-long action that was to go down in history as the 'Great Marianas Turkey Shoot', American fighters and anti-aircraft fire destroyed no fewer than 400 Japanese aircraft as the enemy made frantic and suicidal attempts to attack the US invasion fleet in the Philippine Sea.

That morning, David McCampbell led eight Hellcats from the USS *Essex* to intercept a formation of forty bombers, escorted by twenty Zeros. Leaving five of the Hellcats to tackle the fighters, McCampbell dived on the bombers with his wingman and another pilot, personally shooting down four of them while trying to get at the leader. He finally worked his way through to the front of the enemy formation and shot down the Japanese leader too, despite the fact that his guns kept jamming. The air battle lasted just fifteen minutes, and when it ended the Japanese formation was scattered all over the sky. Altogether, the eight Hellcat pilots had claimed 21 victories for the loss of one of their own number. That afternoon, McCampbell shot down two more Zeros which were attempting to attack a pair of air-sea rescue seaplanes in the middle of picking up some Navy pilots who had been forced to ditch. That brought his score for the day to seven, and the overall tally for the pilots of Air Group 15 was 68.

Five days later, this score was equalled by a single fighter squadron, VF-2, operating from the USS *Hornet*. At 06.00

hours on 24 June, two days after the Battle of the Philippine Sea ended, Task Group 58.1 launched a long-range fighter sweep against the island of Iwo Jima. It comprised 48 Hellcats, including fifteen from VF-2. South-east of the island, the Americans encountered about 100 Zeros, and in the fierce air battle that followed the Hellcats of VF-2 destroyed no fewer than 33 enemy fighters. Three Zeros were shot down by Lieutenant Robert R. Butler, who was leading the squadron, while Lieutenants (jg) R.H. Davis, R.W. Shackford, M.W. Vineyard and E.C. Hargreaves shot down four each. The total for the fighter sweep as a whole was 68 Zeros destroyed for the loss of only four Hellcats, one of them belonging to VF-2.

While the Hellcats were on their way back from Iwo, the Japanese launched a torpedo attack against the carrier task group. Eight Hellcats of VF-2 were flying CAP over the *Hornet*, and they intercepted the torpedo-bombers while the latter were still several miles short of their objectives. In less than five minutes the American pilots shot down eighteen of the enemy, Ensigns Paul A. Doherty and John W. Dear claiming three and the other pilots two apiece. The Japanese tried later that day, this time with a strong fighter escort, but they fared no better. VF-2 tackled them again and sent sixteen flaming into the sea, several of the pilots who had been in action over Iwo Jima that morning adding to their scores. That brought VF-2's total number of confirmed victories in the day's fighting to 67, a record for a Navy fighter squadron in a single day. The squadron lost only one Hellcat.

Of the pilots mentioned above, Hargreaves became an ace on 24 June, with five kills before the day's end. He later increased his score to 8½. Ralph Davis went on to claim 7½ kills, Shackford 6, and Dear 7, some at night.

The battle for the Philippines saw the combat debut of the man who was to rise to second place in the US Navy's list of aces: Lieutenant Cecil E. Harris, who flew Hellcats with VF-18 on the USS *Intrepid*. He opened a spectacular combat career on 13 September 1944 by shooting down four aircraft in a Japanese formation trying to attack the American ships. On 12 October he got four more while taking part in the early series of strikes on Formosa, and on 29 October he repeated the exploit. On this occasion, VF-18's Hellcats were escorting the *Intrepid*'s torpedo- and dive-bombers in an attack on Clark Field, in the

Philippines. The Japanese contested the raid fiercely, sending up a large number of fighters. Harris caught the first two flights of Zeros on the climb and shot one enemy fighter out of each flight, and in the course of the battle he shot two more Zeros off the tails of Hellcats. His eventual score was 24 aircraft.

But it was David McCampbell who retained the top place, and on 24 October 1944 he achieved the most extraordinary combat feat of his career. On that day, the USS *Essex* was one of seventeen US carriers providing air support for the American landings at Leyte, in the Philippines. McCampbell, whose score now stood at 21, was launched from the *Essex* with his wingman, Lieutenant Roy Rushing, and five more Hellcats in response to an incoming bomber alert. The seven fighters headed for Luzon, and before long sighted twenty Japanese dive-bombers heading towards the American fleet. There was as yet no sign of enemy fighters, but McCampbell shrewdly guessed that they must be around somewhere, so he ordered the other five Hellcats to engage the bombers while he and Rushing flew top cover.

Suddenly, a formation of 40 Zeros came into view, several thousand feet higher up. McCampbell and Rushing climbed hard towards them. Amazingly, the Japanese pilots made no attempt to break formation and swarm on the heavily outnumbered Americans, but continued to hold their course. The two Hellcat pilots, still climbing, each selected a target and opened fire: two Zeros went spinning down in flames. Still the Zeros made no attempt to attack, but instead formed a defensive circle. McCampbell and Rushing climbed above them and waited, aware that sooner or later the Zeros would have to break away for lack of fuel.

They waited for ten minutes, then all at once the enemy circle split up and the Zeros straggled away towards Manila in ones and twos. The two Hellcats went after them, and what followed was one of the strangest and most one-sided combats in the history of air warfare. In a running fight lasting just over an hour, McCampbell shot down no fewer than nine of the enemy fighters, while Rushing destroyed four and another Hellcat pilot who joined in got two.

David McCampbell, who was awarded the Congressional Medal of Honor for this exploit, went on to score four more victories in November, bringing his final total to 34. Roy

148

Rushing's final score was 13. Both men returned to the United States when Air Group 15's tour of operations in the Pacific came to an end on 14 November 1944.

The drive towards aerial victory in the Pacific, however, was by no means all attributable to the United States Navy. Squadrons of the United States Army Air Corps (later United States Army Air Force), the Royal Australian Air Force, the Royal New Zealand Air Force, the Royal Air Force and the Fleet Air Arm also played their part.

At the beginning of 1943 there were nine American and two Australian fighter squadrons in New Guinea. Most were equipped with the Curtiss P-40 Tomahawk, but the American units were beginning to receive the twin-engined Lockheed P-38 Lightning. The first to do so was the 39th Fighter Squadron, 35th Fighter Group, at Port Moresby. Technical problems delayed the Lightning's combat debut, but in its first major engagement with Japanese aircraft on 27 December 1942, the 35th FG claimed fifteen destroyed without loss.

The Lightning's main asset was its long range, which made it very useful as a bomber escort. It could also be useful in other ways, too, as was ably demonstrated on 18 April 1943, when P-38s of the 339th Fighter Squadron, operating at extreme range from Guadalcanal, intercepted and destroyed the aircraft carrying Japan's Admiral Isoroku Yamamoto on a visit to Japanese bases in the Bougainville area. In addition to the Betty bomber carrying Yamamoto, the Lightnings also destroyed two more Bettys and three Zeros for the loss of one of their own number.

Two months later, on 16 June 1943, the 339th FG intercepted a large force of Aichi D3A Val dive-bombers and Zeros. One of the Group's pilots, Lieutenant Murray J. Shubin, destroyed five of them to become the only P-38 'instant ace' of the Pacific War. Shubin went on to gain a total of eleven victories; he survived the war only to be killed in a road accident in 1956.

The top-scoring USAAF ace – and, indeed, the leading scorer of any American pilot – gained all his 40 victories while flying the P-38 Lightning. He was Major Richard I. Bong, who became an ace on 5 January 1943 when he shot down his fifth enemy aircraft. He was then flying with the 39th Fighter Squadron of the 35th Fighter Group, but three days later he transferred to the 9th FS of the 49th FG, and it was with this unit that he was to do most of his combat flying. By November 1943 Bong had 21 victories, gained in the bitter air fighting over Milne Bay and Rabaul, and by the following April his score had risen to 28. In April 1944 he was sent back to the United States for a long gunnery and instruction course, and on his return to combat later in the year he destroyed a further twelve Japanese aircraft over the Philippines. He got his fortieth victim, a Nakajima Ki43 Oscar, on 17 December 1944.

In the following month, Dick Bong was once again sent home. On 6 August, 1945 – the day the atomic bomb fell on Hiroshima – he was killed while flying a Lockheed P-80 Shooting Star, America's first operational jet fighter, at Burbank, California.

The second top-scoring American pilot, Major Thomas B. McGuire, also flew P-38s, rising to fame in the Pacific with the 475th Fighter Group. On 26 December, 1944, McGuire destroyed four Zeros over Los Negros in the Philippines to bring his score to 38, only two short of Dick Bong's total. On 7 January 1945, he was leading a patrol of four Lightnings on an offensive mission against the enemy airfield at Los Negros when a lone Zero was sighted. The Lightnings dived on the tail of the enemy aircraft, which was painted a glossy black. The Zero pilot waited until the Americans were almost in range, then flung his aircraft into a tight left-handed turn that brought him on to the tail of McGuire's wingman, Lieutenant Rittmeyer. A short burst, and Rittmeyer's P-38 went down in flames. The Zero turned easily inside the other three Lightnings, and in an effort to get at him McGuire committed one of flying's deadly sins: he attempted a tight turn at low speed. His P-38 stalled and plunged into the jungle, killing its pilot.

Had he lived, McGuire might have gone on to better Dick Bong's score; but in the battles over the Philippines during those closing months of 1944, two other Lightning pilots were climbing rapidly up the aces' ladder. They were Colonel Gerald R. Johnson and Colonel Charles H. MacDonald, respectively commanding officers of the 49th and 475th Fighter Groups. In October 1944 both Groups were operating from Leyte, and there was keen rivalry between their two commanders. On 7 December 1944, MacDonald destroyed three enemy aircraft – Mitsubishi J2M Raiden fighters, known by the Allied code-name of Jack. Still congratulating himself, he took off on a second mission later in the day. Suddenly, Gerry Johnson's voice came up over the radio. Probing inland, Johnson had spotted three Nakajima Ki43 Oscars below him.

'There are three Oscars down below,' Johnson told his wingman. 'Count them – one, two, three.' Almost before the wingman had finished counting, the third Oscar was blazing among the trees.

Gerry Johnson scored 22 kills before being returned to the United States early in 1945. Sadly, he was killed in a flying accident two months later. Charles MacDonald finished his war with a score of 27, fifth among the USAAF aces.

The Supermarine Spitfire also played its part in the Pacific air war, forming part of the air defences of northern Australia. In 1942, after Japanese carrier aircraft had first attacked Darwin, three squadrons of Spitfires had been shipped to Australia at the urgent request of the Australian Government. The three squadrons – Nos 452 and 457 RAAF and No 54 RAF – were formed into No 1 Fighter Wing, RAAF, under the command of Squadron Leader Clive Caldwell, a highly skilled and experienced fighter pilot who had already gained twenty victories in the Middle East.

The Spitfire variant that was sent to Australia was the 'tropicalised' Mk Vc; in a turning fight, or in the climb, it was outclassed by the Zero fighter, as the pilots of No 1 Fighter Wing were soon to learn. In February 1943 the Japanese re-opened their bombing offensive against northern Australia, on the 6th of that month Flight Lieutenant R. W. Foster opened the Spitfire's scoreboard in the theatre by shooting down a Mitsubishi Ki46 Dinah reconnaissance aircraft 35 miles off Cape Van Diemen. On 2 March, Caldwell – now a wing commander – destroyed a Zero and a Nakajima B5N Kate torpedo-bomber, while Squadron Leader A. Thorold-Smith, commanding No 452 Squadron, also shot down a Zero. The latter pilot was killed on 15 March, when the Wing intercepted fourteen Japanese aircraft over Darwin and claimed seven enemy for the loss of the four Spitfires.

The first major battle occurred on 2 May, when the Japanese sent in a force of eighteen bombers and 27 Zeros from Timor. The Japanese were detected by radar while they were still a long way out to sea – 49 minutes' flying time from the coast, in fact – and the Wing's 33 Spitfires were all airborne within fifteen minutes, climbing hard to meet the raiders. When the Spitfires reached 26,000 feet, however, Caldwell saw that the Japanese formation was still about 4,000 feet higher up. To attack it on the climb would have been suicidal, for the nimble Zeros would have had all the advantages, so Caldwell delayed while his Spitfires got into position above the enemy, with the glare of the sun behind them. This meant that the Japanese were able to bomb Darwin without meeting any fighter opposition, a fact that later caused a big outcry in the popular press, but Caldwell was quite right in his decision.

Caldwell's Spitfires, unseen against the sun, shadowed the Japanese until they were out over the Timor Sea, then he ordered No 54 Squadron to attack the Zeros while the other two Squadrons took on the bombers. The Spitfires went into the attack almost vertically and a furious air battle developed as the Zero pilots, recovering from their surprise, turned to meet the attackers. When the battle was over, five Zeros had been destroyed, but only one bomber; and on the debit side, five Spitfires had been shot down, two of the pilots being killed, and five more had been compelled to make forced landings after running out of fuel.

In the weeks that followed, however, Caldwell continued to develop the Wing's tactics, ignoring the growing storm of criticism about the celebrated Spitfire's lack of success, and one day in July 1943 his efforts paid dividends. On that day, No 54 Squadron was scrambled to intercept a raid on Darwin by 47 bombers and their fighter escorts. Only seven Spitfires reached the attackers, but they shot down seven enemy bombers, and two Zeros for no loss. Then, on 20 August, three Japanese reconnaissance aircraft appeared over Darwin, heralding another raid; the Spitfires shot down all three of them. The Japanese sent another; it was destroyed by Clive Caldwell, his 28th and last victory. The Japanese sent yet another, this time under strong fighter escort. No 54 Squadron was scrambled to intercept, and the Zeros fell on the Spitfires as they climbed, shooting down three of them. But the Spitfires in turn destroyed one Zero and damaged two more so badly that it is almost certain they came down somewhere in the Timor Sea.

Soon afterwards, the Japanese daylight raids on Darwin ceased, and the enemy switched to sporadic night attacks which were to continue, with little effect, until early in 1944. Caldwell's Spitfires had achieved their objective.

Early in 1945, the Allies marshalled their air and naval forces for the final drive towards the Japanese home islands. An essential preliminary was the capture of the island of Okinawa, and it was during this bitter campaign – when the US Navy suffered some of its most grievous losses from Japanese Kamikaze suicide attacks – that the Navy's third-ranking fighter ace, Lieutenant Eugene A. Valencia, scored his greatest success. Valencia had already flown one combat tour, destroying seven enemy aircraft, and when he returned to the combat area with Fighting Squadron VF-9 in the spring of 1945 he had a thorough grasp of Japanese fighting tactics. He found three other pilots who were willing to practice his own tactics to perfection, and turned them into a formidable fighting team; their names were James E. French, Clinton L. Smith and Harris Mitchell. The team went into action for the first time over Tokyo in February 1945, and immediately proved its efficiency by shooting down six Japanese aircraft.

On the morning of 17 April, the four pilots set out to strafe Japanese Kamikaze bases on Kyushu, but en route they encountered between twenty and 30 Japanese fighters. The Americans had the height advantage, and Valencia put his combat tactics into practice with dramatic results. The four Hellcats dived on the enemy in pairs, in line astern, making one brief firing pass and then climbing to repeat the process. In a matter of minutes, they sent fourteen Japanese aircraft burning into the sea. Valencia himself claimed six, French four, Mitchell three and Smith one. On 4 May, off Okinawa, the team claimed eleven more victories, followed by a further ten on 11 May. When the four pilots ended their combat tour, Valencia had a total of 23 kills, French eleven, Mitchell ten and Smith six.

The British Pacific Fleet, designated Task Force 57, with the aircraft carriers HMS *Victorious*, HMS *Implacable*, HMS *Indefatigable* and HMS *Indomitable*, was also present for the final assault on Japan. Its fighter squadrons were equipped with Hellcats, Corsairs, Fireflies, and Seafires, and on 1 April 1945, flying a Seafire of No 894 Squadron, Sub-Lieutenant R. Reynolds – who had already destroyed two German aircraft during operations in the North Atlantic – shot down three Zeros to become an ace. The first Fleet Air Arm pilot to reach the ranks of the aces in the

Pacific Theatre alone was Lieutenant D.J. Sheppard, a Corsair pilot with No 1836 Squadron, who claimed his fifth victim – a Yokosuka D4Y Judy – on 4 May. In July, Lieutenant W.H.I. Atkinson, flying a Hellcat of No 1844 Squadron, was one of a group of pilots who intercepted a formation of Aichi B7A Grace torpedo-bombers, Japan's newest combat type. He destroyed two confirmed and possibly a third, adding them to at least two aircraft destroyed earlier in the year, and so became the second Fleet Air Arm ace of the Pacific with at least 5 to his credit.

On 15 August 1945, following the dropping of the atomic bombs on Hiroshima and Nagasaki, Admiral Halsey, commanding the US Third Fleet, ordered the cessation of all offensive air operations. When the order reached the task forces off Japan, the first strike of the day was already hitting air bases near Tokyo. The rearmost wave consisted of the Grumman Avengers of No 820 Squadron, Fleet Air Arm, from the British carrier HMS *Indefatigable*, which were attacked by about fifteen Zeros in the target area. The Japanese fighters were immediately overwhelmed by the Avengers' escort, the Seafires of Nos 887 and 894 Squadrons, who shot down eight of the enemy for the loss of one of their own number.

It was the last time that fighters met in combat during the Second World War.

INDEX

155

French, James E. 153

He111 2–7, 12–13, 17–23, 26, 31,
39–40, 50, 52, 68, 70, 91, 94,
118
He115 17
He177 55
He219 58, 65–66
Held, Sgt Alfred 1
Heligoland 9–10, 119
Henderson Field 137–138, 142
Hennon, Capt William J. 83
Henschel:
126 26–27, 32, 53, 91
129 131
Merrmann, Maj Hajo 61
Hesepe 115–116
Heyer, Lt 112–113
Hill, Tex 80
Hiroshima 137, 150, 154
Hitler, Adolf 47, 59, 61, 114, 134
Holland 51, 54, 59–60, 64, 66, 76,
104, 107, 114, 117
Holloway, Bruce K. 81
Hood, HMS 1
Hornet, USS 146–147
Houzé, Lt 33
Howard, Maj James H. CMH 81,
109–110
Howarth, Sub-Lt R.B. 73
Hull, Flt Lt C.B. 19–20
Hungary 130, 132

I.

Idritsa 123
Ihlefeld, Herbert KC 47
Illustrious, HMS 69–70
Ilyushin:
Il–2 Shturmovik 125–126
Imam:
Ro.37 90
Implacable, HMS 153
Indefatigable, HMS 153–154
India 76, 79–80
Indomitable, HMS 72, 153
Intrepid, USS 147–148
Isle of Wight 45
Italian Air Force 97–98

Italian Expeditionary Air Corps 97
Italy 34, 69–71, 83, 86, 88–90, 94–95,
97–98
Ivanov, Lt-Col Vladimir P. 122–123
Iwo Jima 147

J.

Jacobs, Flt Lt H. 54
Jacobsen, Plt Off L.R. 21–22
Jade Estuary 9–10
Jameson, Gp Capt P.G. DSO 24, 117
Jamieson, Flt Lt George Esmond
56–57
Japan 41, 73–85, 93, 109, 123, 131,
135–154
Japanese Navy, Imperial 81, 135,
139–141
Java 82–83
Jenkins, Lt D.G. 74
Jeram, Sub-Lt D.M. 69, 72
Jever 10, 48
Johnson, Sqn Ldr D.V. 89
Johnson, Col Gerald R. 150–151
Johnson, Gp Capt Johnnie 92, 107
Johnson, Maj Robert S. 106
Johnstone, Flt Lt A.V.R. 'Sandy' 2, 5
Judd, Lt-Cdr F.E.C. 73
Junkers:
Ju52 19, 86–88, 118, 127
Ju87 'Stuka' 5, 20, 23, 40–41,
70–72, 92–95, 99–101, 118, 126,
128, 131
Ju88 1–2, 4, 7, 19–23, 32, 38–40,
50–53, 55–56, 59, 68, 71–72,
91–92, 95–96, 118, 124–125
Ju90 19
Ju188 57–58

K.

Kai-shek, Chiang 76, 80
Kain, Fg Off James Edgar 'Cobber'
DFC and Bar 12–13
Kalinowski, Sgt 59
Kammhuber, Col Josef 49, 58–61, 65

164